THE COLONIAL HERITAGE
OF LATIN AMERICA

THE COLONIAL HERITAGE
OF LATIN AMERICA

Essays on Economic
Dependence in Perspective

STANLEY J. and BARBARA H. STEIN

New York
OXFORD UNIVERSITY PRESS

OXFORD UNIVERSITY PRESS

Oxford   London   Glasgow

New York   Toronto   Melbourne   Wellington

Nairobi   Dar es Salaam   Cape Town

Kuala Lumpur   Singapore   Jakarta   Hong Kong   Tokyo

Delhi   Bombay   Calcutta   Madras   Karachi

To those Iberians and Ibero-Americans who have had the courage to speak out against irrationality and injustice.

The colonial relationship . . . chained the colonizer and the colonized into an implacable dependence, molded their respective characters and dictated their conduct.

A. Memmi, *The Colonizer and the Colonized*
1965

In politics it is a mistake to believe that abuses must be remedied slowly and gradually. . . . Timidity in correcting abuses can only stem from two considerations: either because neither evils nor causes are well understood; or to avoid offending those who, interested in maintaining the very abuses, are therefore opposed to the common weal; to put it more clearly, those who prefer their personal interest over the good of all.

Campomanes, *Apéndice a la educación popular*
1775

Introduction

The most striking feature of contemporary Latin America is its economic dependence, underdevelopment, or backwardness with respect to the North Atlantic world. No less striking a feature is the internal chasm between wretched rural communities and glittering metropolises, between primitive and sophisticated technology, between poverty and luxury, between starvation and abundance. In economic dependence and its syndrome of economic and social polarization we find the principal heritage of three centuries of subordination to Spain and Portugal. Another century and a half of national existence has seen the persistence of economic dependence and internal social dichotomies despite the emergence of independent governments republican in form and responsive in theory to an indigenous popular will. Thus Latin America *appears* ready to bequeath to the future the legacy of the past.

This pessimistic prognosis has only the semblance of truth. For beside the traditional structures and often within them are evident today signs of forces unreconciled and in fact irreconcilable with the past. The growing impact of technology within and without Latin America operates in numerous and often contradictory ways to create new expectations and a readiness to reject the past in order to realize an inescapable if uncertain future. It is not the realm of this volume, however, to describe the present or forecast the future but rather to suggest the origins of the evident travail of change which confronts Latin America today.

This volume is not micro-history of Latin America. It is a series of essays probing for those features of Latin America's past—their metropolitan and colonial origins and development, and their projection into the nineteenth century—which may provide an understanding of the process of change in the area. The essays are limited in focus and the approach is frankly economic and social. The authors view Latin America as a continent of inadequate and disappointing fulfillment and seek to pinpoint the co-ordinates of sustained backwardness in examining the process of economic change in a dependent, peripheral, or colonial area. Within broad chronological periods and representative regions the focus is upon certain basic institutions, patterns of behavior and attitudes which have had impressive continuity in Latin America: hacienda, plantation and associated social patterns, mining enclaves, the export syndrome and related trade mechanisms and mentality; elitism and racism; nepotism, clientelism, and a tradition of private right in public office.

We are grateful to generous colleagues—William Cline, Charles Griffin, Shane Hunt and Arno Mayer—for criticism, and to Iska Fraidstern and Sheldon Meyer of the Oxford University Press for editorial assistance.

Pitfalls in analysis and synthesis within the compass of simplicity and brevity are obvious, particularly so when Latin American economic and social history have yet to be developed. Objections will undoubtedly be raised to generalizations made, terminology employed, and elements omitted. It is hoped, however, that the essays will clarify and provoke. *La grandeza del hombre es el flechazo, no el blanco.*

B.H.S.
S.J.S.

Princeton, New Jersey

Contents

PART ONE

1500–1700

CHAPTER I

Europe and the Structures of Dependence, 1500–1700

1

In 1492 Spain and Portugal were economic dependencies of Europe and, despite their creation of overseas empires in the sixteenth century and their control of such areas until about 1824, they remained dependencies. This anomalous status as colony and empire shaped the history of the Iberian countries and their colonial possessions. It conditioned colonial society, economy, and politics, and indeed the course of Latin American history to modern times.

The subordinate role of the Iberian monarchies as Atlantic powers was abundantly clear by 1700 to Englishmen and Frenchmen as well as to their Spanish and Portuguese contemporaries. That year, when the death of Charles II initiated a contest for the control of Spain and its dominions in Europe and America, provides a watershed from which to assay the relative positions of the Atlantic nations intimately involved with the western hemisphere.

2

*John Bull—"Shall I serve Philip Baboon [Philip V of Spain]
with broadcloth, and accept of the composition that he offers,
with the liberty of his parks and fish-ponds?"*
                        John Arbuthnot, *Law is a bottomless pit, or
                        the History of John Bull,* 1713

Of the western European nations emerging from late medieval times between 1500 and 1700 England had undergone the most radical transformation in economic and political structures. In two hundred years its population had grown from 4 to 5.8 millions, attributable in part to an agricultural revolution based upon new food and forage crops, new techniques and significant changes in land tenures. While a powerful aristocracy with large landed estates still existed there, that aristocracy had few inhibitions about joining forces with aggressive, enterprising merchants, miners, and shipowners. From the sixteenth century on, gentry and merchants had jointly invested in corporate overseas enterprise, and London as both administrative and commercial center had facilitated this interpenetration.

During the seventeenth century—that "century of revolution" for England—a mercantile elite and groups associated with it had established hegemony in a parliamentary government to advance its purposes while providing a forum for dissent. The sense of "national will" thus effected was responsible in great measure for the creation of the expanded financial resources necessary to support the growing economic and political power of England. Obstructions to economic development were reduced or removed: royal, aristocratic, and corporative privilege, monopolies, prohibitions, tolls, and price controls. Factors promoting development were strengthened: the joint-stock company, the Bank of England, the spread of religious tolerance, and the advance of science.

England's growth resulted largely from internal structural reforms and national policies concerned for the most part with trade and manufacture. By 1700 England had moved far beyond its earlier role of mere producer of export staples. It had curbed raw wool exports, imported artisans, forged its own textile industry. "The cloth trade is England's Indies" it was said, for the merino wool and dyestuffs imported from Spain and Portugal were returned to the peninsula as textiles for consumption there or for re-export to the colonies; Iberian gold and silver flowed to England to compensate for the deficit in the Iberian balance of trade and were re-exported to purchase luxury items from the Far East demanded by European consumers. By a series of navigation acts England had developed a merchant marine able to challenge the Dutch. The significance of these measures was not lost on contemporaries, one of whom characterized the Act of 1660 as "a true way to enlarge dominions throughout the world, the most easy for conquests, and the least costly for appropriating the property of others."

In the course of the seventeenth century England, a latecomer to empire, had acquired outposts in Asia, Africa, and America. Colonization of the Atlantic seaboard of North America and the acquisition of Jamaica (1655) and other Spanish islands in the Caribbean provided outlets for slaves and manufactures, and sources of naval stores, sugar, dye-stuffs, and silver. Thus the last half of the seventeenth century saw the emergence of two mercantile interests trading with the Spanish empire: those carrying goods to Spain for domestic sale or re-export to its colonies, and those trading to the West Indies from where goods penetrated the Spanish dominions.

By 1700, then, England had made a breakthrough into what we now call the modern world. The transformation of its society and economy, the interpenetration of aristocracy, gentry, and merchants, the prestige and authority accorded to powerful commercial interests, the expenditure on ship-building and the expansion of the royal navy, the mobilization of national resources and manpower for the extension of trade and access to raw materials profitable for the carrying trade—these by 1700 had led Britain to probe the perimeter of what the English and other western European commercial powers recognized as the greatest real and potential source of raw materials, consumer markets and, above all, supplies of gold and silver bullion and specie: the colonial empires of Spain and Portugal in America.

The significance of the Iberian nations and their American colonies as profitable market and source of raw materials in forging English pre-eminence can easily be overlooked. In a variety of ways the English, Iberian, and Ibero-American economies were interlocked by 1700.

In the first half of the seventeenth century, the English woolen textile industry based upon coarse cloths produced under guild controls and marketed by an oligopoly of export merchants—the "old" drapery—was in crisis. During the preceding century English woolens had been sold in a seller's market in northern Europe; by the beginning of the

seventeenth century competition from Dutch, Silesian, and
Venetian manufacturers contracted the exports of this leading sector of the English economy. Inflation in England, by
raising wages, reduced competitive advantages of its producers and favored Europeans mobilizing non-guild labor.
English response to the shift from a seller's to a buyer's
market evolved during the seventeenth century as producers
developed a new variety of cheap woolens, the lighter and
less durable "new" drapery or "Spanish" cloths—so-called because the first products utilized fine, short staple Spanish
wool. Such cloths were manufactured outside the guild
towns of south-central England, and the middlemen were
financed by London merchants. Ultimately these woolens
were sold to consumers in the Mediterranean and especially
in Spain and Portugal and their American colonies, areas
hitherto offering limited demand for heavy woolens. It was
the marketing of such woolens in the Mediterranean that
led to the growth of the English carrying trade between that
area and northern Europe.

Moreover, English entrepreneurs associated with the new
manufacture were found in the vanguard of the seventeenth-century revolution which in turn opened new avenues of penetration into the Spanish empire in America. The
abortive Providence Island Company, followed by the seizure of Jamaica, were designed for colonization but also to
serve as contraband entrepôts; thus the new cloths benefited
from the effective achievements of Cromwell's and his associates' Western Design for opening the Caribbean. Textiles,
first woolen, later cotton, whether carried to Africa to exchange for slaves, to Cadiz for silver to exchange at Calcutta
for calico, or contrabanded on Caribbean shores for dyewood and silver, were to be England's key to economic

development and its challenge to the European continent. It is difficult to understand much of what went on in Spain and Portugal, England and France, Europe and America after 1600 without taking into consideration the competition of cloths in the customs houses and on merchants' counters of the new and old worlds.

3

> *"The French complain that fortune has not given them America. They are mistaken. What Indies are there for France but Spain itself!"*
>
> Baltasar Gracián, *El Criticón,* 1651

> *". . . the greater the merchandise carried to the Spaniards, the more ingots and piasters from the Indies are returned to us. . . . His Majesty wishes that the Marquis de Feuquières should particularly apply himself to maintain and increase this commerce by every means the merchants may suggest to him."*
>
> Louis XIV, *Instructions* for the Marquis de Feuquières, Ambassador to Spain, 1685

France was also competing for control of the trade with the Iberian world. But in the quickening growth of Europe from 1500 onward France's pace of growth was well behind that of England. Despite France's greater endowment of agricultural resources and larger population (her population hovered around 20 million in the seventeenth century) geography imposed obstacles to her development as a modern state; the definition of national frontiers long absorbed material and human resources. An impressive military establishment (about 400,000 men under arms in 1700) and a

large supporting bureaucracy became important factors in
the modernization of France in contrast to the English experience. A many-layered and numerous aristocracy that held
commercial enterprise to be derogating to noble status continued in the seventeenth century to occupy high place in
army, province and court. When co-operation between monarch and monied groups provoked reaction in the Fronde in
the mid-seventeenth century, aristocratic influence was diminished but far from liquidated. Indeed, the French bourgeoisie long continued to cherish aristocratic ideals and often
abandoned trade at the first opportunity to achieve aristocratic status. As a consequence, economic progress and state
polity were executed largely by an enlightened bureaucratic
elite under the auspices of a monarch who strove toward
central executive power but who in fact acquired initiative
by balancing powerful factions—not always successfully.

In the second half of the seventeenth century, in response
to events in England where a rival far more formidable than
the Dutch was emerging, the French under Colbert undertook to modernize their economic structure by tax reform,
systematic protection of industry, state-imposed production
norms, government-supported industries emphasizing luxury production, chartered trading companies, and the creation of a navy and merchant marine. By the century's end
however, manufacture and trade were still hampered by the
prevalence of tolls, privileges, tax-farming, sale of office, and
by involvement in expensive Continental wars.

Well before 1700 the French government had encouraged
its merchants and manufacturers to enter the Iberian trading
area. France was Spain's largest single supplier of imports,
but in America, despite probes and persistent privateering,
no permanent foothold of value was established until 1697

when Spain accepted French dominion over eastern Hispaniola or Saint Domingue.

In 1700, however, the French had to utilize means other than territorial aggression and contraband to maintain their position in Spain and its colonial areas. Besides the evident disparity between English and French seapower it was recognized that an attack on the brittle structure of the Spanish empire would touch off the collapse of the Spanish patrimonial state, thus endangering not only French access to peninsular markets but the borders of France itself. Thus, just as at home French domestic growth was initiated within the framework of existing institutions and without revolutionary upheaval, so the defense of French economic interests abroad against English pressure in Spain and America lay in the preservation and utilization of the Spanish colonial system rather than in its destruction. Hence French insistence on placing a Bourbon on the Spanish throne when Charles II died in 1700. To the bureaucratic elite of the reign of Louis XIV a French-guided reformation of Spain's internal and colonial administration promised to eliminate a major weakness in the Spanish colonial system: contraband with France's competitors, the English in Jamaica and the Dutch in Curaçao. Unity against England, fortified by dynastic bonds, was to bring a "natural" alliance of the Spanish and French Bourbons during the eighteenth century.

4

*". . . although those who came to America were vassals of the
Kings of Spain, who could produce unity between a Biscayan
and a Catalan who come from such different provinces and
languages? How can an Andalusian get along with a Valen-
cian, a man from Perpignan with a Cordoban, an Aragonese
with a Guipuzcoan, a Gallician with a Castilian, an Asturian
and a man from the Montaña with a Navarrese?"*

Oviedo y Valdés, *Historia general y
natural de las Indias*, 1535

*"And so the fact that there is neither money, gold nor silver
in Spain, is because there is; and the fact that Spain is not
rich, is because she is; making two true and contradictory state-
ments about one subject, Spain."*

Gonzalez de Cellorigo, *Memorial de la
política necesaria*, 1600

By 1700 not only was Spain's last Hapsburg monarch mori-
bund, but so was its economy. The War of the Spanish Succession over the conflicting claims of Hapsburgs (supported
by Holland and England) and Bourbons to the Spanish
throne merely spotlighted what had long been apparent in
the courts and counting-houses of Europe. As early as 1624
Francis Bacon had examined the "brittle State of the Great-
nesses of Spain" and concluded that "their Greatnesse con-
sisteth in their Treasure; their Treasure in their Indies; and
their Indies . . . but an Accession to such as are Masters by
Sea." Spain, he observed, was "thin sowne of People" and
"exhausted by so many Employments in such vast Territories as they possesse" to the degree that it was a "kind of

Miracle to see ten or twelve thousand native Spaniards in an Army."

At the end of the seventeenth century there were one million fewer peninsular Spaniards than at the beginning, and in 1715 Spain's population was roughly what it had been in 1541: 7.5 million. The loss of people was due to a number of causes natural and man-made: plagues and epidemics took a toll as they did elsewhere in Europe; colonial conquest and development absorbed more Spaniards than official registers indicate; military garrisons in Europe drained young men of marriage age; and the expulsion of Jews and Moors and the flight of New Christians and later Moriscos represented an outflow of important constituents of population. Population decline, however, was only one aspect of a more generalized phenomenon of particular significance for colonial development: economic contraction.

Spain's regression or "decline" from first to third rank among European powers during the seventeenth century deserves definition in both its economic and political context. With the discovery and conquest of America and union with the Hapsburg empire in the sixteenth century, Spanish *dynastic* wealth and prestige grew enormously in Europe. The dramatic decline of this wealth and prestige impressed Europe profoundly in the late seventeenth century as royal "coffers" were found empty, navy and merchant marine without ships and men, royal army without soldiers and equipment, and the throne itself without effective incumbent. A legend of Spanish wealth and prestige had become incorporated into the everyday language of Europe: a *Peru*, an *Indies*, a *Potosí*, a Spanish lord or *grandee*. When Bacon argued for war with Spain he understood that he must first destroy illusions of Spain's strength.

Perhaps the greatest myth assimilated into European thinking of this period was the myth of "Spain" itself. In the late fifteenth century Spain had scarcely begun to consolidate its political geography and internal structure as a nation-state. Further, the acquisition of empire in the sixteenth century resulted not only in the atrophy of the process of consolidation but in proliferation of the Iberian patrimonial political structure. In this process political and economic forces abetted each other. The marriage of Ferdinand and Isabella, often considered the birth of the modern Spanish state, resulted not in the unification of the kingdoms of Aragon and Castile but in condominium in which the two parts of the "Spanish Crown" co-existed as separate entities with separate laws, taxation systems, coinage, and trading patterns. In turn each kingdom aggregated politically and economically disparate parts. While this pattern of political growth was common in late medieval Europe, its persistence in the early modern age leaves Spain in the rear-guard of west European political development.

The most fateful event in the development of the Spanish patrimonial state was the aggregation of an empire in America to the crown of Castile as a kind of fief or personal possession on the premise that Columbus sailed as the personal agent of Isabella. In consequence the kingdom of Aragon and its subordinate areas of Catalonia, Naples, Sicily, Mallorca, and Valencia were legally barred from direct exploitation and administration of the New World. A third political subdivision of the Iberian peninsula, the Basque provinces, was merely associated with the Castilian crown through an allegiance which Basques held to depend upon recognition of local privileges including freedom from Castilian taxation and military recruitment and most striking of all, maintenance of a customs frontier which gave the "tax-exempt provinces" the status of foreign nation in trade with Spain. Thus Basques too had no direct contact with America. It is not surprising that Spain was frequently referred to as "the Spains."

A second significant development was union with the Holy Roman Empire under the Hapsburgs on the accession of Charles V. With reason European jurists pondered the validity of a Spanish-dominated "universal empire" in the sixteenth century. If Ferdinand was the "first prince of Christendome," and Charles was more so, even Machiavelli's handy rules of thumb for princes were of doubtful use in the effective control of so large a patrimony. And yet proliferation of dynastic patrimony was another factor in the decline of Spain. Perhaps the illusion of grandeur, the myth of control, was the most salient element in the façade of the Spanish monarchy. Yet in time even the appearance of power would be scratched and found illusory.

The military impact of the Spanish monarchy on the Renaissance world was spectacular; its performance in consolidating the economic and political basis of that power in Spain was far from impressive. In 1492 Spain was a dependency of Europe, exporting wine, wool, iron ore, and other primary products. In the first half of the sixteenth century national output expanded in response to colonial demand for food, clothing, and hardware; but this growth was soon nullified by the wide and persistent price differential between peninsular manufactures and those of the rest of western Europe. The influx of American silver, spectacularly after 1550, inflated the Spanish price structure more rapidly and profoundly than that of its trading partners and in the process ruined the few industries which had developed

before 1550 to meet the new colonial demands during conquest and early settlement. The textile industry of Valencia,
Sevilla, Toledo, Avila, Segovia, and Burgos collapsed under
the pressure of the mass of cheaper woolens and silks from
northern Italy, France, Holland, and England. When silver
shipments from America began to decline sharply around
1630 little infrastructure of domestic industry existed in
Spain.

Spanish agriculture, like Spanish industry, also experi-
enced a short-lived stimulus from rising prices and demand
at home and in the colonies; in response, labor and investment shifted from the center of the country to the southern
periphery. In the latter half of the sixteenth century wheat
and wine output in central Spain failed to meet demand,
while coastal areas expanded production of oil and wine for
export at the expense of the small holder. The estates of the
great wool-, wine-, and oil-producing magnates of Extre-
madura and Andalusia grew in size and importance while
the agricultural areas of Old Castile were abandoned.

With the contraction of domestic manufacture, the development of export agriculture on the southern periphery of
the peninsula, and the persistence of natural and artificial
barriers to internal trade, foreign and colonial commerce
became the lodestone of the peninsular economy. The establishment of the court at Madrid (1561) initiated a lucrative
trade in luxury goods with Italy, France, and Flanders. By
the end of the seventeenth century the so-called Five Major
Guilds of Madrid supplying imported luxury goods dominated the economic life of the capital. The trade of Madrid
depended to a large degree, however, upon the remittance of
the "royal fifth" of the products of American mines and of
customs receipts and profits of the colonial trade concentrated in the port of Sevilla.

Trade with the colonies, described in a later chapter, was from the beginning organized to assure a monopoly of benefits to the Crown, subjects, and residents of Castile. Controlled by a Board of Trade (*Casa de Contratación*) and a merchant guild (*Consulado*), the colonial trade reflected the narrow exclusivism of late medieval commercial practices. In the course of the sixteenth and seventeenth centuries this structure and practice received sanction in a body of heterogeneous laws ultimately compiled in "Laws of the Indies," the legal instrument to which Andalusian monopolists appealed in defense of their privileges and practices until the end of the colonial era.

Notwithstanding law and royal intent, however, foreigners participated in the American trade from its outset, and by 1700 guild members were for the most part mere fronts for Genoese, French, Dutch, and English resident and nonresident merchants. Increasingly, foreign vessels conveyed merchandise to colonial ports and foreign naval squadrons convoyed the treasure fleet home. Contraband in port and collusion in custom house helped bring Spain's colonial trade to its nadir at the end of the seventeenth century.

The social repercussions of these economic changes were far-reaching. Although the land remained the livelihood of most Spaniards, during the bonanza of the sixteenth century those with funds to risk or with will to follow "the unquiet trade of merchandizing" could enrich themselves by trade with or in the Indies or in the importation of luxury goods. Gentry lacking a respectable income could acquire fortune and status in the many employments connected with the control of trade at its key points in the peninsula, along its line of entry and transit in the colonies, and in the mining centers from which payment was drawn. Finally, those unable or unwilling to avail themselves of these avenues to security could invest their savings in annuities, government bonds, and church funds and so guarantee themselves a modest income.

In the seventeenth century, as industry and agriculture declined in the interior of Castile, population migrated to the south, to Madrid and to other cities where poor Spaniards could gain a precarious livelihood in the service of the well-to-do, in petty trade, or as beggars depending finally on the charity of church, merchant, and aristocrat. In the course of these two centuries, the ranks of aristocracy, bureaucracy, and church expanded as families sheltered their fortunes and secured their future in a variety of entailments, in life annuities, ecclesiastical benefices and the purchase of inheritable public office. Aversion to manual trades, ingrained since the Reconquest, was further fortified while the ideal of an aristocratic life-style came to dominate Spanish life as well as its literature. To a greater degree than elsewhere during these two centuries Spanish merchants sought status and security for themselves and their offspring in land and title, in other forms of income-producing property, and in public preferment. Inflation and extravagance often enough canceled the purpose of entailed inheritance and made new recourse to the "remedy whereunto . . . such as are broken in their Estates commonly have Recourse; to wit, to go for the Indies, the Refuge and Protection of all your Spendthrifts, and desperate People of Spain." With luck a new competence might be achieved but though the cycle was repeated and the *indiano* and *perulero* became familiar figures in Spanish society, no cumulative benefit accrued to the economy of either Castile or the rest of the peninsula.

Within the contracting economy of the seventeenth century an institution of traditional importance in the Mediter-

ranean world—the family—took on new significance. From
the level of ruling dynasty to that of the most humble
bureaucrat, family relationships were matters of economic
survival. "Alliance and kindred" are key words to Spanish
society of this period for upon such relationships depended
in great measure access to livelihood and wealth and status.
Even the close relationships represented by common regional origin are to be understood in part by kinship for
within regions, especially in the populous valleys of northern
Spain, community and family were closely related. Bureaucracy was particularly structured to receive the strong imprint of family interests and pressures as those in office
sought favors for relative-*paisanos* in public post or private
employ. Merchants depended first and foremost on kinship
to secure loyalty and secrecy among business associates and
dependents. Family networks extended so widely throughout Spanish economic and political life that certain families
at certain periods could count on having representatives at
many strategic points: in key ministries and posts of the
Madrid bureaucracy, in army, navy, church, and trade in
Spain and America. Granted that such patterns tended to
break down in time, or in crossing the Atlantic, it was also
true that other extended families tended to replace them.

In viewing Spain and its colonial empire as a whole over
the two centuries before 1700 it is apparent that underdeveloped areas cannot easily modernize their economies
and transform traditional societies of aristocratic values and
aspirations. Certainly not in the case of Spain and Portugal
which, at the onset of their imperial experience, were imper-
fectly organized, export-oriented, and lacking a national
bourgeoisie or merchant capitalist group capable of stimulating indigenous growth. Spain might have utilized its

resources, manpower, and institutional structures to develop a flourishing commercial seaborne empire. It might have entered rapidly upon a stage of accelerated commercial capitalism as did Holland, England, and France between 1500 and 1700. It could be argued that Spain might have seized church property as did England to develop internal resources and might have reorganized huge landed estates via tax policies to increase revenues.

The record shows, however, that Spain of the epoch of the Reformation was not prepared to break with its late medieval heritage. Centuries of territorial expansion on the Iberian peninsula, the Reconquest, the struggle against Moslem culture had emphasized the role of the militant aristocracy and the church militant. The medieval heritage seemed no impediment to Spanish expansion before 1500; it appeared, on the contrary, a factor of unity and growth. The exploitation of the American colonies, Mexico and Peru, made the restructuring of the Spanish semi-feudal, land-based, aristocratic economy and society unnecessary. The process was more than atrophy, however, for if essential productive sectors shriveled, certain consuming sectors—aristocracy, bureaucracy, the service occupations, the church—burgeoned. The resulting symptoms of pathology were apparent in government as in society and economy, in the new as in the old world. After 1600 when the modernizing states of Europe were questioning concepts and practices of privilege, of the "absolute state," of the church militant, of private usufruct of public power, of bullion rather than production as wealth, these institutions and attitudes took new root in Spain and Spanish America.

5

"The two cities of Lisbon and Oporto may be justly considered the two eyes of Portugal for here centre the whole riches of the country and all their trade with foreign nations, and their own possessions in the Brazils; upon which last especially depends their whole existence as a people, and the immediate support of the throne."

Arthur W. Costigan, *Sketches of Society and Manners in Portugal*, 1787

If Spain was the sick man of Europe in 1700, Portugal was the forgotten man. A colonial dependency of western Europe in 1500, Portugal was two hundred years later a virtual dependency of England if we are to judge by the terms of the Anglo-Portuguese treaty of 1703, the Methuen Treaty which linked the Portuguese metropolitan and Portuguese colonial American economies to that of England. Methuen brought Portugal and its colony in Brazil into a web of economic imperialism whose center was England.

At the end of the fifteenth century, on the eve of the great overseas expansion of the Iberian nations, Portugal was relatively unified, had a population density somewhat greater than that of Spain, although in absolute terms its population was far less, and for over a century had been under a monarchy attuned to the aspirations of the small, interrelated bourgeoisie of its principal commercial hub, the city of Lisbon. To Portugal via Lisbon flowed grain, metallurgical products, woolens, and salt fish from northern Europe in Low Country vessels, and from Lisbon flowed back African

gold and the salt of Setubal. The ties of economic dependency were clear.

For over a century the Portuguese had probed the Atlantic
westward to the Azores and southward along the west African coast to the Madeiras and the Cape Verde islands seeking direct access to the gold mines of Monomotapa. They
maximized their technology of the sea, creating a school of
navigation, training seamen, collecting information about
the west African coast, seeking an all-water route to exploit
the trading potentialities of the Indian Ocean and the Far
East. The first to round the southernmost tip of the African
continent, the Portuguese concentrated their limited resources in capital, manpower, and shipping to exploit their
maritime breakthrough to India, the Malacca Straits, and
South China. And once masters of the Indian Ocean they
dominated that vast sea's maritime shipping routes including the carrying trade between Japan and China and exploited a virtual monopoly, first of the trade in spices, later
of the trade in such luxuries as silks and porcelains in return
for silver.

It is no wonder that during the first half of the sixteenth
century the Portuguese considered the discovery of Brazil
(1500) as a matter of secondary importance. In fact, efforts
to consolidate control over the seaboard of what is now
Brazil, roughly between the present ports of Santos and
Recife, were largely a reflex action taken to prevent France
and England from establishing competitive coastal enclaves
for the export of Brazilian dyewood used in the manufacture
of woolens in the Low Countries and England. Only the
fear of competition in the dyewood trade on the Brazilian
coast led to sustained occupation in the latter half of the century and the establishment of a plantation economy. The

development of sugar estates in the coastal fringe between Salvador and Recife stemmed from the actions of a handful of Portuguese entrepreneurs who enslaved Amerinds to work their plantations. When this labor proved inefficient and scarce, the Portuguese undertook the first large-scale recruitment of labor from west African ports to Brazilian sugar and tobacco plantations, that is, the forced migration of Negro slaves via the slave trade. It proved as impossible to establish Portuguese emigrants as small-scale farmer-colonists in Brazil as it was to create comparable enclaves of emigrants in Spanish America.

In the Indian Ocean and along the Asiatic coasts the Portuguese excelled as creators of trading enclaves and as shippers. In historical perspective their activity represented the last phase in the medieval commercial pattern developed by Italian maritime centers. The gains from the Eastern trade were, it appears, not transferred to investment in Brazilian plantations, nor in the carrying trade of Brazil, nor even in the creation of sugar refineries in Portugal. At the end of the sixteenth century, the Dutch controlled about 66 per cent of the shipping between Brazil and Portugal, the Dutch owned a large share of the sugar exported from the colony, and Amsterdam not Lisbon had about twenty-five sugar refineries utilizing semi-processed Brazilian sugar (1621).

A fortuitous conjunction of relatively advanced maritime technology and geographical location permitted the late medieval or pre-capitalistic economic structure of Portugal to expand into the Ocean Sea. It did so on the basis of the old commodity trade utilizing light, high value items which required only a few heavy tonnage vessels. It was only a matter of time before a more developed area of west Europe, the Low Countries, would mobilize larger resources of man-

power, capital, and shipping to follow the Portuguese to the
source of their trade and to eject them. In the first fifty years
of the seventeenth century the Dutch forced the Portuguese
to cut back operations on the periphery of Asia and in Brazil
they seized and held Recife thereby controlling the sugar
trade, if not the growing of sugar, between 1630 and 1654.
Nor did the Spanish occupation of Portugal between 1580–
1640 provide adequate resources to protect Portugal's foothold in Brazil. Although the Portuguese recovered Recife in
1654, Brazil's sugar monopoly was already broken by English and Dutch plantation development in the Caribbean.

By 1700 two centuries of Portuguese overseas expansion
and contraction left only the illusion of greatness while the
gains of trade were reflected neither in metropolitan manufactures, nor financial institutions, nor population growth.
In fact there had been a high rate of emigration first to the
commercial enclaves in Asia and later to the agricultural
fringe in Brazil. Colonial revenues had only expanded the
Portuguese service sector. In the War of the Spanish Succession a weak Portugal allied itself with England, on England's terms, to survive the threat of Franco-Spanish invasion.

The Methuen Treaty (1703) obliged Portugal to reduce
tariffs on woolen imports from England, reductions later extended to woolen imports from France and Holland. In return, England granted favored treatment to Portuguese
wines over those of France and Spain. In 1700 roughly 11
per cent of all British exports flowed to Portugal and its colony in Brazil. Portugal, a tiny metropolis with a huge
American colony, was incapable of supplying the colony's
major imports of textiles and metallurgical products, and
unable to pay for domestic imports without colonial prod-

ucts. Like Spain, Portugal was already an appendage of its colony in America. In other terms, through the early capitalist economy, society and political structure of Portugal, Brazil was linked to the west European economy. Brazil was the economic core of Portugal.

Until now we have used the watershed of 1700 as a vantage point to review a process of change in the relative position of west European states over two hundred years. In those years the dependent or economically dominated nations of the Iberian peninsula expanded overseas, creating in turn dependent trading areas without substantial feedback. They failed to modernize internal structures which might have altered their subordination to the dominant economies of England, Holland, and France. It has been seen how England, confronted by economic crisis caused by falling demand for its principal export, responded by adaptation and innovation. France, too, long dominated by Holland and then challenged by England, initiated changes in economic and political structures. Holland, challenged at sea by the English and on land by the French became Europe's banker, a role she played effectively until the Napoleonic age.

Description, however, is not entirely adequate in analyzing the causes and effects of these changes. In examining England's performance in the seventeenth century and beginning of the eighteenth century, what seems obvious is that she had no overwhelming superiority in technology, commercial, industrial, and maritime, over her Dutch and French rivals. What *is* evident is the readiness of the English to become aggressors, to utilize their geographical position and maritime experience to formulate an offensive strategy which they employed repeatedly against the Spanish, the Dutch, and the French. The English opened the way to empire in the New World by commercial drive, industrial innovation, and finally by resort to the instruments of war. War was that ultimate instrument of policy which the English skillfully employed to accumulate a mercantile fleet practically overnight, and to extort concessions from the defeated. Underdeveloped nations should not overlook the fact that the English amassed a mercantile fleet from the seventeen-hundred-odd merchant vessels seized as prizes from the Dutch in two years (1652–54). They were not the only nation to act in this way, but they were the most successful. The English, it would appear, had taken note of Bacon's policy-recommendation on "Lucrative and Restorative *Warre*." From the mid-seventeenth century onward they forced the Spaniards and the Portuguese to yield tariff concessions on imports of English goods and to strengthen the position of their resident merchants at Lisbon and Sevilla. Economic imperialism, then as now, requires collaboration, and the Iberian elites both aristocratic and mercantile had perceived in the course of the seventeenth century that within the status of economic dependence it was possible to preserve intact or nearly so the life-style to which they had become accustomed.

CHAPTER II

The Colonial Economy

1

"Trade is the sacrifice of the Rich and the Poor; those engaged in it achieve the level of profits they desire, without effort and without stepping out of their Houses; the abundance of ships arriving at Veracruz gives them no cause to cheapen goods they hold in the Capital because the Wealthy and Powerful monopolize goods to the prejudice of those who are not, and by storing them in their Warehouses they price them as they wish and exploit the rest of Humanity. There is no Control. This Capital is a City in name only, and is really only a Hamlet."

> Viceroy of Mexico, Duque de Linares,
> to his successor, 1716

The Spaniards took seventy to eighty years to occupy what was to be their empire in America. They spent about two hundred years of trial and error in establishing the essential elements of a colonial economy tied to Spain, and through Spain to western Europe. By 1700 these elements were (1) a series of mining cores in Mexico and Peru, (2) agricultural and ranching areas peripheral to the mining cores developed for the supply of foodstuffs and raw materials, and (3) a commercial system designed to funnel silver and gold as specie or bullion to Spain to pay for goods produced by western Europe and funneled through one Spanish port for distribution to the American colonies. But to most Spaniards and their descendants in America in 1700, the glorious days lay far in the past, during the time of conquest, the organization of subject peoples, the creation of a vast bureaucratic apparatus and, above all, the discovery and exploitation of the richest silver mines the world had ever known. The golden age of Spain was a time of conquest, not peace; of silver, not gold.

2

". . . they began to populate these mines rapidly, and the first settlers were soldiers located nearby, and then in response to news of silver there began to come many people from Mexico, and among them merchants with goods."

Alonso de la Mota y Escobar, *Descripción de los reinos de Nueva Galicia*, about 1602

During the first two hundred years of colonial rule, the Spaniards developed a colonial mining sector to maintain the metropolitan economy and Spain's international position in western Europe. Within a twenty-year span, 1545–65, the major mining strikes in Mexico and Peru were made. The mining cores required relatively large amounts of Indian labor, which was conveniently located within mobilization distance of the mines. Drafted Indian labor (*mitas*) moved periodically to the mines, then were permitted to filter back to their communities of origin as new drafts replaced them. The horrors of mita labor constitute a vast literature of exploitation.

Mining operations required, of course, more than labor. The workers needed housing, stores, churches, saloons. The mines required pit props, masonry, winches, ladders, and vast quantities of leather. They required mules and horses not only in the towns and mines proper but also to move bullion outward to mints and to points of export, and to move supplies inward from plantations and ranches, and from coastal points which received European goods required by the mining centers: iron and steel tools, luxury items, and above all, mercury used in the amalgamation of silver from crude ores. Mining also created a domestic market for colonial production of both woolen and cotton textiles by individual artisans and in sweatshops. Despite prohibitions, this production expanded since the import-export wholesalers handled only the high-priced fine woolens and silks obtained either from western Europe or the Far East.

Working capital was always the mineowners' weak point. They turned to the many church endowments (*obras pías*) or they borrowed from and frequently entered into partnership with merchants who, more often than not, ended in full control of the mines they had originally financed. Risk-bearing in mining was always great.

The characteristics of this frontier mining economy can easily be imagined. For the Spaniards there was the opportunity to exercise the essential entrepreneurial functions—risk and ruthlessness—in the hope of a bonanza and return to the homeland to become a newly enriched, newly titled aristocrat. Here was one of the great rewards of conquest: social ascension and status in less than a lifetime of diligent work and careful economy at home. To be sure, many mineowners remained in America. Some failed, others preferred to put their savings into nearby estates to raise foodstuffs and cattle. This became more general after about 1610 and accelerated during the seventeenth century, the century of economic contraction in America as in western Europe.

The mining boom of the period 1545–1610 is a classic example of private entrepreneurship in which miners, merchants, and the state collaborated and shared the returns. Miners and merchants in America, the merchants of Sevilla and through them the merchants and manufacturers of western Europe all profited directly or indirectly. State participation took the form of a percentage (about 20 per cent) of silver mined and minted, and the profits of mercury distribution which remained a state monopoly farmed out to merchants. Indirectly, the state profited from the duties on goods exported to America and the specie received from America at Sevilla and re-exported to western Europe to settle the balance of payments for Spanish and Spanish-American imports. As the leading sector of the colonial economy mining paid for the administrative costs of empire, the ecclesiastical and secular officials high and low, viceroys, judges (*oidores*) of audiencias, governors and captains-general, local officials such as *alcaldes mayores* and *corregidores,* military garrisons, not to overlook the royal navy's escort vessels accompanying inbound and outbound convoys.

3

"*. . . it is the custom for all owners of haciendas, workshops, estancias and drovers to sell their workers along with their establishments.—What? Are these Indian laborers and servants free or slave?—No matter. They belong to the hacienda and must serve on it. This Indian is my master's property.*"

Jerónimo de Mendieta, *Historia eclesiástica indiana,* 1595–1596

"*Then the Indians had no sickness; they had no aching bones; they had no burning chest; they had no abdominal pain; they had no consumption; they had no headache. At that time the*

course of humanity was orderly. The foreigners made it other-
wise when they arrived here."

                    The Book of Chilam Balam of
                    Chumayel, late seventeenth century

The export orientation of the Latin American economy—
still its dominant characteristic and one of its principal heritages—was a product of the first two hundred years of Spanish colonialism and of the mining boom on the Mexican
plateau and in the Central Andes where agricultural technology and population density had produced advanced cultures. There the Spaniards opened mines, and there they
created subsectors of the mining nuclei, large estates devoted
to agriculture and ranching.

In an era of primitive mining technology, the Amerinds'
agricultural surpluses, skills, and manpower ensured the
success of Spanish mining enterprise. Introduction of the
mining economy acted as a cutting edge of west European
capitalism; its success helped literally to cut down indigenous population and to cut apart pre-conquest agrarian
structures. On their ruins Spaniards created the hacienda.

The hacienda developed before 1700 to supply the mining
economy and to permit the Spanish entrepreneur of conquest to re-create in America the status symbol of southern
Spain, the landed estate with a largely immobile labor force.
The conquest of Sevilla and the occupation of Andalusia in
the thirteenth century permitted the Spanish nobility to
carve out wheat-, olive-, and vine-growing estates. The conquest of America brought the same pattern, but in the
process the centers of Amerindian civilization, their cultures,
and their population collapsed.

In areas of arid climate so-called early or ancient civilizations have emerged in terms of population growth, eco-

nomic specialization, and urbanization through man's mastery and application of the technology of water control—irrigation agriculture. In the semi-desert areas of Mesoamerica and the Central Andes, without plow or wheel, draft animals or animal transport, man increased food supply by harnessing water and by organizing manpower. The incentive to abandon extensive and nomadic cultivation of low and unstable yields for intensive, sedentary agriculture of high and dependable yields was clear. According to recent calculations, slash-and-burn agriculture in Central Mexico requires 1,200 hectares per annum to furnish an adequate food supply for 100 families; intensive *chinampa* or lake platform agriculture in the Valley of Mexico requires only a fraction of this surface, between 37 and 70 hectares.

Intensive agriculture developed in the Mexican highlands and Central Andes over at least three millennia before 1500 and seems to have reached the limits of existing New World technology and productivity between 1200 and 1500 in the formation of the Mexican or Aztec "state" centered in the Valley of Mexico and the vaster Inca "empire" of Peru. It culminated in a highly sophisticated labor-intensive agriculture which produced a principal foodstuff, maize or Indian corn (in the higher regions of Peru and Bolivia, the potato and another tuber, quinoa) and in ancillary crops of beans, squash, tomatoes, and chili peppers. Skillful agriculturists in the Valley of Mexico offset the disadvantages of inadequate and fluctuating rainfall by utilizing the water of melting mountain snows and by maximizing the huge natural basin of interlocking lakes; in Peru they utilized the rivers of mountain valleys and the water flows through valleys along the dry Pacific coast. Water was harnessed for agricultural ends by canal irrigation which in turn demanded high inputs of manpower for elaborate terracing, often on steeply inclined valley slopes, for digging and facing canals and for their upkeep. Spanish observers of the sixteenth century were quite properly and understandably impressed by the engineering skill of the peoples of the Central Andes, just as twentieth-century agronomists are impressed by archaeological evidence of techniques for diverting water from valley to valley in pre-conquest times. In the Valley of Mexico, Spanish observers marveled at the dike system created and maintained to keep brackish water from flowing into sweet water areas, and the intensive chinampa agriculture.

Such an agricultural economy favored demographic growth. In the Central Andes the Amerindian population may have been between 3.5 and 6 (some say 10) million in 1525. For all Central Mexico (1519) recent demographic analysis suggests a figure as high as 25 million. Periodically in the millennium before 1500 as population pressed upon food supply, interregional conflict led to conquest and to the consolidation of agricultural communities into blocs which created special cultural expression in architecture, in rectilineal urban ceremonial and administrative centers, in ceramics, weaving, sculpture, in methods of time-keeping and accounting, in religious focus and practice. Periodically, such irrigation civilizations collapsed followed by the diffusion of their material and intellectual culture, their reappearance in subsequent patterns forged by new cultural centers.

Agricultural sophistication was reflected in increasing stratification, i.e. in the formation of hierarchies: nobility, soldiers, and religious elite, a group of merchants and skilled artisans producing for the demands of the elite, and a mass of agriculturists. The expansion of one community at the expense of its neighbors, the forging of hegemony in the form of annual tribute payment or incorporation into an integrated empire, meant pressure upon the agriculturists at the base of the economy and society, and produced periodic revolts, sometimes successful, sometimes not. In the century before the conquest, the irrigation civilizations which Spaniards encountered in the Valley of Mexico and the Central Andes were dominated by an elite increasingly militarized, obviously expansionist, generally ruthless toward deviants within or without their societies. While the Aztec elite periodically subdued recalcitrant dependent areas by military expeditions which imposed or reimposed tribute, the Inca elite simply uprooted troublesome communities and resettled them for more efficient control. The pattern of expansion and militarism, the signs of social stratification, the attempts by the elite to mobilize and appropriate economic surplus of their own and their subject peoples, suggest that at the moment of west European eruption into Middle and South America the limits of available agricultural technology had been reached and as in the past, large aggregations of communities were about to fission again into constituent communities as a result of demographic expansion and inelastic agricultural output.

Expansion, stratification, and exploitation developed mechanisms other than military force to maintain internal cohesion. Long before the Spanish conquest, religious sanctions and goals also furnished a kind of social cement. In both irrigation cultures, the priesthood occupied a key social function, organizing the agricultural cycle, indoctrinating the young, marking with appropriate rites the passage through the life-cycle from birth to death, facilitating the incorporation of new communities by religious syncretism, giving meaning and purpose to existence, fortifying the strong, and comforting the underprivileged. From the economic surpluses of land communally owned and farmed the Amerindian priesthood received allocations just as did the military and the aristocracy. The ruthlessness with which Spaniards sought to extirpate the practice and symbols of pre-conquest religious thought suggests the effective role played by the Amerindian ecclesiastical establishment. The Amerind's strong religious commitment, his deference to religious omniscience and authority, his theologically sanctioned submission to the hardship, suffering, and frustration of a peasant existence in a harsh world merged with the Catholicism imposed upon him to form another component of the colonial heritage.

What was essential to the creation of Spanish hegemony, the forging of the colonial mining and agricultural-ranching economy, above all, to the development of the hacienda was the Amerind's tribute to society in the form of payments in kind or in labor. Conquest gave the new aristocracy—the Spanish overlords—immediate access through *encomienda* both to food supplies and to a large labor force organized to render specialized services to their new rulers: tribute in the form of local produce or craftsmanship, labor on public works. Long before the great mining strikes of the mid-sixteenth century the leading entrepreneurs of conquest demanded payment for their personal outlay on equipment and risk-taking in the form of Indian tribute, Indian labor and royal grants of land. Cortés, quite appropriately, carved out for himself and his descendants huge land grants and claims to Indian tribute and services, and there were plenty of emulators in his unruly retinue.

Spaniards going to the New World left a society of landholding aristocrats, a small bureaucracy, a few townsmen, and a mass of peasants and estate laborers. It was logical that they refuse to create family farms in the colonial world where there existed huge expanses of land and a large population of skilled, subservient Amerindian agriculturists—both land and labor the spoils of conquest. Immediately they laid claim to labor and to food supplies; in a word, they exploited the Indians as vassals of the Spanish monarchy. Indians plowed, cultivated, and harvested the lands of the new Spanish overlords. Since at first there were in America no draft animals, Indian porters by the thousands moved goods from point to point on their backs.

The immediate aftermath of conquest and occupation of the more densely populated areas of Amerindian civilization was catastrophic. A combination of epidemic disease (smallpox, measles, typhoid), overwork and resultant physical debilitation, and culture-shock induced by the remolding of a communal society along individualistic, profit-oriented lines produced in the sixteenth and early seventeenth centuries one of the most disastrous demographic declines in world history. Between 1492 and about 1550 what we may term the conquest complex literally annihilated the indigenous population of the first areas of west European and Amerindian culture-contact, the Caribbean. It decimated the population of Central Mexico where a population recently estimated at about 25 millions in 1519 was down to something over one million in 1605. In the Central Andes, where studies of historical demography are few, the general pattern of demographic disaster following west European occupation seems to have been repeated. A population of perhaps between 3.5 and 6 million in 1525 is believed to have declined to 1.5 million by 1561 and to have continued to fall to a level of .6

million by 1754. Culture shock in the sixteenth century, cor-vée labor or the mita in mines in the sixteenth and seven-teenth centuries, and debt peonage in the eighteenth century form the currently accepted sequence of factors accounting for the decline of Amerindian population there.

The demographic disaster in America undoubtedly was a prime factor in the mining recession that developed in Mex-ico and Peru after about 1596 and which endured in Mexico for about a century. Mining output dropped steadily and the repercussions spread throughout the nearby and distant estates which had developed around the mining cores to provide corn and wheat, beans, fodder, mules, burros and horses, pork, mutton, hides, and coarse textiles.

Miners and merchants shifted investment to land and ac-celerated the formation of the latifundium. Without the in-centive or stimulus coming from the mines, their output of silver, labor force and dependents, the large estates tended to become relatively self-sufficient. For the economic and social elite, mineowners, estate owners, ranchers, the major preoc-cupation became the maintenance of an adequate and reli-able labor supply. Nearby Indian communities were pres-sured to supply labor by appropriating their land or by encouraging residence on estates by advancing small sums for tribute and tithes. Once resident, Indians received further advances for food and drink, for sacraments of baptism, marriage, and death. Debt peonage became a principal form of labor recruitment and maintenance. More than the cash nexus tied the landowner-patriarch to his semi-servile de-pendents. The hacienda became a place of refuge for the Amerind who found pressures on his community unbear-able. He found a kind of security in the hacienda complex. To his hacendado-patriarch-judge-and-jailer he offered his labor and his fidelity. In return he received daily rations, primitive medical treatment, religious consolation, and an established inferior position. The hacienda as unit of production and as patriarchal social nucleus was to survive as a colonial legacy in Mexico until 1910 and even later in Guatemala, Ecuador, Bolivia, and Peru. The Amerindian communities also managed to survive in an expansionist, capitalistic, monetized economy and society by perpetuating tradition, language, dress, and group consensus as effective bulwarks against the pressure of the White man's world for Amerindian land and labor—a pattern familiar to students of reservation Indians in the United States.

4

"Slaves are the hands and feet of the sugar mill owner, because without them, in Brazil it is not possible to found, maintain and increase a plantation, nor to operate a mill."

". . . Brazil is inferno for Negroes, purgatory for whites, and paradise for Mulattoes and Mulattas."

João Antonio Andreoni, *Cultura e opulencia do Brasil*, 1708

The landed estate oriented toward export—the second element of the colonial heritage of Latin America—bloomed in the Spanish empire in America only in the eighteenth century, and then in peripheral colonies such as Cuba, Venezuela, and the basin of the Rio de la Plata. It was Portuguese America's role in the seventeenth century to create a prototype of plantation export agriculture in America. For the Brazilian sugar estate or *engenho de açucar* represented a form of economic activity independent of mining which was the *raison d'être* of the hacienda in Mexico and Peru. It forged a pattern of economic organization and society, an agro-social complex that was reproduced and adapted in the Caribbean at the end of the seventeenth century and in the southern colonies of the British empire in North America in the eighteenth century.

The plantation is the second variant of the large estate in America. Historians, social anthropologists, and economists have in recent decades groped for working definitions of the hacienda and plantation, although they recognize that often the two overlap. In Spanish America, they point out, the hacienda was an estate of large dimensions raising grains or cattle. Their products were consumed locally at the mining cores or large urban centers such as Mexico City and Lima. Amerinds constituted the labor force, dependent, relatively immobile, constrained by a special form of wage labor, debt peonage.

Originally the word plantation referred to the transfer and settlement of Europeans in an overseas area. By the end of the seventeenth century the plantation had become an estate in tropical or sub-tropical zones, specializing in one crop, utilizing a dependent, immobile labor force of chattel slaves exported involuntarily from Africa. Unlike the hacienda, the plantation was an independent economic unit created to produce staples for external, that is, European consumption. It was the product of European technology applied by European technicians for European entrepreneurs; it was often financed by European capitalists who also provided for its production, shipping and insurance, final processing, distribution, and marketing facilities. Like mining, the plantation was a New World enterprise whose stimuli were entirely European. From Brazil to Virginia, the plantation in America very early displayed features which still distinguish it. It specialized in one crop, utilized income from exports to import goods and services which its specialization made prohibitively expensive to furnish locally: foodstuffs, metallurgical products, and particularly luxuries. It was a prime example of economic specialization.

The full-blown prototype of plantation agriculture in America, the seventeenth-century Brazilian *engenho,* was the Portuguese instrument of effective occupation and settlement. It was perhaps the most significant colonial legacy to the area. The engenho, to be sure, emerged from a series of experiments as the techniques of sugar growing and processing migrated from the Mediterranean to the Atlantic islands —the Azores, Madeiras, Cape Verdes, and Canaries—and ultimately to the Brazilian south Atlantic coast between Santos and Recife. Sugar estates had appeared on the island of Hispaniola in the Caribbean before 1530, but they did not become large-scale sustained exporters to Europe. Yet as early as 1498 Portuguese sugar from the Madeiras was being warehoused for sale at Antwerp.

In Brazil, Portuguese entrepreneurs and their Low Country backers encountered favorable conditions: a coastal strip of excellent black soil easily worked once cleared, adequate rainfall, which eliminated the irrigation required in the Atlantic islands, and low transport costs from estates to shipping centers at Recife and Bahia. One factor of production, however, was lacking: an abundant, docile, sedentary labor force. Gradually the Portuguese entrepreneurs expanded slaving operations against nomadic Amerinds along the Brazilian coast, and to protect them the Jesuits constructed separate communities which, despite their intentions, only served in practice to prepare their Amerindian charges for ultimate incorporation into the expanding plantation system, first as food suppliers, then as chattel slaves. Brazil's semi-nomadic Amerinds proved inefficient as a plantation labor force, and the Portuguese proceeded to mobilize west African labor. In the sixteenth century they shipped about 50,000 chattel slaves to Brazil; in the seventeenth century over 500,000. They early recognized the proposition, "No slaves, no sugar, no Brazil." In 1570 there were about 60 engenhos; this number had risen to 346 in 1629 and to 528 by 1710, including small, medium, and large engenhos.

The Brazilian plantation syndrome of monoculture, chattel slavery, and production for export should not be separated from the west European center. The engenho was only another subsector of the European economy in particular of the Dutch economy, since the Portuguese remained mere intermediaries, re-exporting Brazilian sugar shipped often in Dutch vessels, often processed in Dutch refineries and distributed in north, central, and eastern Europe by Dutch merchants. Dutch goods were used by Portuguese slave traders in Africa. The Dutch eventually seized and occupied part of the Brazilian sugar coast around Recife between 1630 and 1654 as an enterprise of the Dutch West India Company. Once ejected by Brazilian planters who mobilized their own resources, the Dutch retreated to the Caribbean taking Brazilian sugar technology and experience to Surinam and Curaçao, from where it was ultimately diffused to the other islands of the Caribbean. There, in the last half of the seventeenth century, the Dutch, English, and French islands soon replicated the sugar plantations of Brazil in pattern and techniques. The division of the Caribbean and the establishment of the plantation were also to form the colonial heritage of that area. By 1700 the Brazilian sugar economy was in crisis as west European consumers turned to the cheaper product of the Caribbean.

The process of estate formation and labor recruitment on hacienda and plantation in the New World between 1500 and 1700 should not be examined solely in microcosm. Specialists in the area tend to focus upon details of the process of post-conquest growth and synthesis, and thus to emphasize the apparent autochthonous elements of the process: the mixing of Iberian, Amerindian, and African elements in America. A macrocosmic view, however, is required to put the process in the perspective of the colonial heritage. One cannot overlook the essential fact that in the period 1500 to 1700 the Ibero-American empires functioned as a peripheral segment of the expanding west European economy. In this function they may be compared to another peripheral area, central and eastern Europe, which supplied the European core with grain, timber, cattle, furs, and ores just as America furnished it with silver, gold, sugar, tobacco, hides, and dyestuffs. Shifts of economic dominance among the Dutch, English, and French did not modify this essential relationship with the peripheral areas. Here the scarce factor of production was labor, and it had to be coerced from the subsistence economy into the export or "open" economy.

Paradoxically, as west European economic development brought social differentiation, mobility, and greater personal freedom to peasant proprietors and urban and rural wage laborers, in peripheral areas of the west European economy labor became more "unfree." In central and eastern Europe it became the "second serfdom." In America it took various forms: encomienda, repartimiento, mita, and ultimately debt peonage and chattel slavery. The Negro was transplanted bodily from an African subsistence economy to a peripheral area of export agriculture. Loss of personal freedom, then, had become by 1700 part of the colonial heritage. This was part of Africa's and Latin America's contribution to the development of liberty in western Europe.

5

"*The fleets to New Spain must leave every two years, for were they to depart annually that Kingdom would not be able to absorb them—of this we have had disastrous experiences to the prejudice of both our trades. And because there is an interval in their sailing, those in New Spain have time to make their arrangements and sales to the internal market, and to receive their value by the time the other fleet arrives. . . . And their volume must be what Your Majesty orders in the manner of former times.*"

Consulta del Consejo de Indias, 1713

"*This way of Trading to the Indies . . . by Whole-Sale . . . is no way prejudicial to Gentility, for we see not only Gentlemen, but the Nobility of Castile deal in the Indies; and it is much to be lamented, that for want of our honouring and encouraging Merchants, most of the Trade is fallen into the hands of Foreigners, who grow Rich, and are enobled with what we despise.*"

Joseph de Veitia Linage, *The Spanish Rule of Trade
. . . Made English by Capt. John Stevens*, 1702
(based upon the Spanish edition, 1672)

"*Without the Indies or its trade, Spain would fall from its greatness, because there would be no silver for Your Majesty, for the ministers, for private individuals, for those holding encomiendas and inheritances, which all comes from the In-*

dies. . . . Were the Indies lost, gone would be the income of
those kingdoms, and Your Majesty must seek a remedy. . . ."
Marqués de Varinas, *Mano de relox que*
pronostica la ruina de la America, 1687

Spain's major colonial problem was how to maximize its control of the silver and gold exported to the metropolis, the basis of Spain's economy and society and the principal support of Spain's European position. Even more important to our analysis of the colonial heritage was the effect that preoccupation with mining had upon the structure and growth of the colonial commercial system.

From the Spanish imperial viewpoint, the underdeveloped Spanish metropolitan economy made all-important control over specie and bullion flows. Such flows provided financial liquidity at a time when public borrowing was both difficult and costly, and when fiscal policies could not quickly be modified. In addition, state finances, the bureaucracy and the military establishment, the nobility drawing pensions from state funds or from colonial properties or investments, monopolies and other privileges, the church establishment deriving income from colonial tithes, estates and lending operations, the merchant middlemen in Sevilla and their foreign merchant creditors and suppliers, the retired merchants, miners and bureaucrats receiving income on colonial investment—all depended on the inbound fleets from the Indies freighted primarily with specie and bullion, registered or illicit. After 1650 a significant percentage of silver, contrabanded or lost to privateers, may never have reached Spain at all; and of that which did, a large proportion never entered the Spanish economy. It was transshipped at Sevilla to settle the balance of trade with French, Dutch, English, and Italian merchants who supplied up to 90 per cent of colonial imports and a large proportion of goods for peninsular consumption. This was one of the prices paid by Spain for failure to create an indigenous commercial bourgeoisie and to develop national production of ironware, steel, nails, textiles, and paper.

Economically backward in 1550 and increasingly so thereafter, metropolitan Spain fell back upon an essentially late medieval commercial system, a sort of mercantilism in one port, Sevilla (after 1717, Cadiz), to profit from its American possessions. Since this system is more often described than explained, it may be useful to view it in perspective before examining its structure. Most European nations, at one time or another in their history, have tried to maximize capital and trading skills by concentrating them in one area, one major port. What is difficult for the modern observer of the Spanish imperial trading system to understand is how this system could survive for 300 years with only minor adjustments. The modern observer is perplexed by the resilience of an imperial trading system providing its manipulators with relatively little feedback in the form of large gains from trade: little capital accumulation, practically no multiplier effect upon metropolitan industrial, agricultural, or banking structures.

The system required control over the mining of apparently inexhaustible natural resources, silver and gold, and a monopoly of distribution of the metals. This monopoly nominally benefited Iberians in America and in the metropolis. At the risk of oversimplification, it may be argued that the structure and function of Spanish imperial trade represents the maximization of the limited possibilities of a backward metropolitan economy. Spanish economic backwardness led to the formulation and application of new control mechanisms, just as the collapse of the international trading system after 1929 led to the propagation of national controls over foreign trade in Latin America and elsewhere. The establishment of formalized structures of supervision—the Board of Trade (*Casa de Contratación*), a merchant guild at Sevilla (*Consulado*), and convoys of escorted vessels (*flotas* and *galeones*)—indicates that the government perceived how vulnerable this system was to foreign penetration and wished to control specie and bullion inflows from its controlled overseas area by exacting "transit tolls" on silver and gold re-export. Since Spanish goods constituted a low percentage of the total value of exports to the colonies, trade was channeled via one port to ensure and facilitate collection of customs duties. The state obtained fiscal gains, while registered Spanish merchants earned income as expediters, not owners, of cargoes, and sometimes as shippers.

At the one authorized Spanish port of Sevilla, the merchant guild and the Board of Trade constituted the main control mechanisms. The guild, dominated by a wealthy minority supervising the entry of new members, sanctioned corporate oligopoly; it excluded not only non-Spaniards, but even non-Castilians. Foreign merchants, although resident and officially recognized in their own corporate bodies with extraterritorial rights, could in theory participate only indirectly in colonial trade as suppliers; in practice, the formal exclusion functioned as ineffectually as do the current corporate arrangements common in most Latin America republics today to impede foreign domination while preserving foreign participation. The Sevilla oligopolists were, at best, intermediaries collecting commission fees. The Board of Trade, a government-appointed trade board whose bureaucrats cultivated intimate ties with resident merchants both

Spanish and non-Spanish, applied control mechanisms through registry of goods, personnel, emigrants, immigrants, and ships and shippers which moved to and from the colonies in scheduled fleets or convoys. Such was the shadow of state control that the government entrusted to the Sevilla guild collection of the fee (*avería*) which was applied to the costs of outfitting and maintaining the armed convoy escorts.

The pattern of commercial centralization was extended to America to facilitate toll collection. At the western terminus of the Atlantic trade designated ports in the Caribbean—Cartagena, Portobello, Veracruz—maintained official contact with the metropolis via Sevilla. Through these ports, like the medieval factories or trading posts which Italian cities had established along the Mediterranean coast, the trade from the hinterland of Mexico and western South America was funneled. At the American trading points merchants applied a pricing mechanism based upon purposeful undersupply, with the price level adjusted to the available purchasing power represented by the silver and gold supply in the hands of the colonial merchant intermediaries gathered for the arrival of the convoys.

Historians have generally been unduly fascinated by the formal features of a complex state-structured and state-dominated trading or commercial system centered on southern Spain with administrative tentacles fanning out to the Caribbean control points and spreading from there to centers of colonial production for export. The colonial commercial system was on one hand the product of the sheer scale of new world geography, size of population, and resource location and, on the other, of the Spanish level of economic development. Trading with America was not like trading with the Low Countries or England in the middle of the sixteenth century; it was not possible to obtain export commodities in the colonies by dispatching merchants to American seaports. America's mineral resources were located deep in the continental heartland and were surrounded by an indigenous population unprepared to exploit them and disinterested in commercial exchange with the Spanish overlords. To have confined the exploitation of the American colonies to a type of English merchant adventurers' organization would have overtaxed the capital and technical resources of Spanish entrepreneurs and, for that matter, of any west European merchants at that time. Furthermore, by about 1550 Spain had to defend her merchant vessels on Atlantic sea-lanes against attack by English and French privateers. In brief, the exploitation of America demanded a political organization far exceeding the resources of a trading company.

The interplay of these factors led to a division of role between the Castilian state and Spanish entrepreneurs. While the state took responsibility and some profit from the creation and maintenance of the political and economic superstructure in the colonies, the merchant, mediating the exchange of goods for silver at key points, controlled effectively the flow of trade and commission fees. The crown sometimes conferred upon the merchant guild, often a large creditor, the functions of government in customs collection and decision-making in affairs affecting its interests, just as the colonial corregidor or alcalde mayor in local government blended private interest and public administration with state sanction.

It is not surprising, therefore, that consulados in colonial trade at Sevilla, Mexico City, and Lima—groups often joined by interest, by regional origins, and by kinship and alliance

—constantly resisted the modernization of the Spanish commercial system. They opposed innovations such as the joint
stock company, which would have been incompatible indeed with conditions of the trade at Sevilla: restricted membership, controlled undersupply of a captive market, secrecy
of operations. Adam Smith later compared the Cadiz mercantile community to a privileged company, but the monopoly of colonial trade enjoyed by the Andalusian port manipulating non-Spanish goods in a captive market could
scarcely be compared to the Merchant Adventurers despite
some superficial similarities. Not until the eighteenth century did privileged trading companies appear in Spain and
then notably to serve areas of agricultural rather than mining development. With few and doubtful exceptions, their
existence was brief, due not only to their own defects but
also to the active opposition of the trade guilds.

Three considerations help explain the permanence of the
colonial trading structure with no appreciable modification
until the end of Spanish colonial control of America. First,
the system was permeable to external manipulation: non-
Spaniards resident at Sevilla dominated colonial trade by
advancing goods or credit or both, and by employing Spanish merchants willing to lend their names to merchandise in
fact wholly owned by foreigners and shipped to the colonies
often under the eye of foreign supercargoes in foreign ships.
The manipulation also took the form of bribery to cover
contraband at every phase of the movement out of Sevilla
and back. At every level of operation foreign interests bribed
seamen, stevedores, customs officials, and Madrid's bureaucrats and ministers. Few officials were impermeable to
bribery.

In the second place, the system's longevity was the result

of its flexibility. The system in practice allowed for greater
participation in colonial enterprise than its closed structure
suggests. Between the state and private Spanish interests
there developed a symbiotic relationship. Merchants financed placemen seeking colonial office, and they provided
loans to bureaucrats proceeding to America on the promise
the placemen would co-operate in the illegal sale of goods
there. At all stages of the colonial bureaucracy, merchants
located officials who countenanced contrabanding, from customs officials to viceroys, including the naval officers
charged with convoy duty. Until 1700 the limited range of
profitable colonial enterprise—the mines and related activities—channeled Spaniards toward trade, *the* sector of opportunity in the colonial economy.

Finally, while the returns on colonial trade to Spanish
guild members at Sevilla were low compared perhaps with
those which flowed to English, Dutch, French, or Italian
suppliers of goods and credits, the Spanish involved were
satisfied because alternate opportunities did not exist. The
rate of return on colonial trade to Spaniards and their associates in Sevilla—a small, privileged group, most of whom
were mere fronts for foreign merchants—permitted a higher
level of income and consumption than other occupations in
Spain.

The Spanish government bestowed privileges and exemp-
tions on this entrepreneurial group in their functional
corporation or guild because this group and its foreign
links offered to an inefficient and penurious government
funds which that government was incapable of obtaining
through taxation of a privileged aristocracy and an ecclesiastical establishment. The silver flows from America made
the Spanish government independent of formal assemblies

or representative groups which, if they granted loans and new taxes, might in return have demanded participation in the legislative process. If American silver distorted the Spanish economy, it emasculated the Spanish cortes, too.

It has often been argued that a colonial system embodies in exaggerated form the virtues and the vices of the metropolitan power. The Spaniards reproduced in their colonies on a vast scale the structural defects of the metropolitan economy. A tiny nucleus of colonial ports handled legal imports and exports. In these ports or their major hinterland points of distribution, a small number of merchants, more often than not related by kinship ties with their Sevilla or Cadiz counterparts, concentrated upon distributing a limited volume of imports at grossly inflated prices in return for silver deliberately undervalued in America. Until long after 1700, they had little incentive to handle bulky colonial exports unless the structure of European demand and the price level there made the effort profitable. In America, the Spanish merchants in league with miners and bureaucrats had no incentive to diversify the structure of exports by stimulating agricultural production or by creating local industry. Such diversification was tolerated but not encouraged. Nor did they develop a colonial fishing industry, nor specialized colonial production for intercolonial trade. The potentialities of interregional trade were neither recognized nor, if recognized, exploited.

Toward the end of the seventeenth century exploitation of the colonial world became increasingly difficult. As long as colonial demand remained within predictable limits, as long as no new areas of colonial export developed, as long as Spain's European suppliers remained content to exploit the colonies through Spain, or as long as direct contraband activities from islands in the Caribbean did not become excessive, the Spanish colonial system of exchanging maximum mine output for minimal luxury imports and discouraging agricultural and ranching exports had reasonable possibilities of survival. But the commercial and industrial revolution of the eighteenth century and the growing aggressiveness of English and French commercial interests soon made it clear that the Spanish colonial system would have to be modified or it would be shattered.

CHAPTER III

Society and Polity

1

"In Spain it is a sort of title of nobility to descend neither from Jews nor Moors; in America skin, more or less white, indicates a man's rank in society."

A. von Humboldt, *Essai politique sur le royaume de la Nouvelle Espagne,* 1807

"The condition [of the Spaniards in America] as conquerors of a conquered land, makes them the first inhabitants, the preferred and the privileged of all America; and woe to us, woe to the peninsula, and woe to the Indies the day we lose our ascendancy, source and sole shield of obedience and subordination."

"The wretched Indian . . . was [at the time of the Conquest] like a filthy animal, wallowing in the trough of the most shameless sensuality, unending drunkenness and the most apathetic slovenliness . . . a mad dog savoring human flesh. . . . Neither the history of ancient times nor tradition has transmitted to our day the memory of so degenerate, wretched and unhappy a people. . . . The Indian . . . en-

56

dowed with.... laziness and languidness ... stupid by na-
ture ... drunk by instinct. ... This is ... the true portrait
of the Indian today. ..."
"[The] castas whose lazy hands are employed in peonage,
domestic service, trades, artifacts and the army, are of the same
condition, the same character, the same temperament and the
same negligence as the Indian. ... Drunken, incontinent,
lazy, without honor, gratefulness, or fidelity. ..."
"[The] whites who call themselves American Spaniards show
their superiority over the ... Indians ... by their inherited
wealth, their career, their love of luxury, their manners and
the refinement of their vices. ..."

The merchants of the Consulado of
Mexico to the Cortes, 1811.

The social heritage of colonial Latin America was not
merely a rigid structure of an elite of wealth, status, and
power at the apex and, at the bottom of a broad pyramid, a
mass of poverty-stricken, marginal, powerless, and subordinate people. Such societies have flourished everywhere.
The tragedy of the colonial heritage was a social structure
further stratified by color and physiognomy—by what anthropologists call phenotype: an elite of Whites or near-
Whites and a mass of people of color—Indians and Negroes,
mestizos and mulattoes, and the gamut of White, Indian,
and Negro intermixture called the *castas*. As North America
has come to perceive, a society may perpetuate social ine-
qualities far more effectively when the maldistribution of income is buttressed by phenotype.

A superficial comparison of Iberian and Ibero-American
society about 1700 suggests that Iberians had managed to re-
produce in the Mexican and Andean highlands and along
the coast of Brazil a replica, or what passed for a replica, of
their Old World society: a two-class or two-stratum social

structure—an elite of landowners, miners, high bureaucrats, and churchmen, a mass of rural dwellers in Amerindian communities or on haciendas or tropical plantations, and between these two strata a small group of merchants, bureaucrats, minor ecclesiastics. In other words, in both areas there existed a social structure typical of an agrarian, preindustrial, or underdeveloped economy. Nonetheless, while in the Iberian peninsula income, status, and power positioned people in one or the other stratum, in the Ibero-American colonies color as well as income, status, and power determined social position.

In Iberian and Ibero-American societies the function of phenotype—and associated with it, "purity of blood" and religion—may be viewed as the outgrowth of Iberians' colonizing and colonializing experiences both on the peninsula and in the New World. The Christian Reconquest, as Cantabrians moved southward, brought the subordination and eventual expulsion of different ethnic groups, Muslims and Jews. During this prolonged expansion two factors were of enduring importance: the rationale of a religious mandate and the material rewards for risk and military expertise. In the subsequent structuring of peninsula society and polity, the criterion of purity of blood—the absence of Jewish, Muslim or Negro ascendants—was associated with that of religion as a perquisite of membership in the political and social elite. Such criteria ensured not only the supremacy of Christianity but also the perpetuation of the Cantabrian families who had spearheaded the Reconquest and profited most by the expropriation of non-Christian property. The Inquisition followed by the expulsion of the Jews, by the later flight of insecure Jewish converts (New Christians), and ultimately by the expulsion of converted Muslims

(*Moriscos*) finally gave the peninsula the semblance of an ethnically homogeneous population.

The conquest of the New World extended the ethos evolved during Reconquest. Subsequent socio-economic change in both peninsula and colonies reinforced the criterion of "purity of blood" or "race" for membership in the elite. At the outset conquest turned Amerinds into vassals, paganism turned them into wards, and "inferiority" or reluctance to accept Christianity and wardship into "people without reason." To be sure, early miscegenation of Spaniards and Amerindian elite women furnished the Spaniards with willing mestizo allies and collaborators; yet the growing number of American-born Spaniards (*criollos*) and of mestizos was soon viewed by Spaniards as a potential threat to their domination. Later, in the seventeenth century, when economic contraction in both America and the Spanish metropolis increased competition for access to wealth, status, and security, the criteria of purity of blood and phenotype were buttressed at home and in the colonies.

The arrival of the Negro chattel slave in Ibero-America added another ethnic factor. His phenotype and legally prescribed inferiority fitted him readily into a society of castes; where Negro freedmen and mulattoes appeared and their social mobility posed a threat to the elite, formal and informal barriers were invoked. While barriers existed to curb the social mobility of all non-Spaniards, those falling upon African ascendance were the most severe and enduring.

By 1700 colonial society in America was, on the contrary, anything but homogeneous. It was indeed a cultural mosaic in which status, income, and power were concentrated among those judged White or Caucasoid, and diluted as one moved down the scale to Amerind and Negro.

2

"The Indian as pure Indian, and the Spaniard as pure Span-
iard, each one in his class is extremely useful to political soci-
ety and it may be said that they are the basis of agriculture, in-
dustry and the arts; but when each one is mixed with the
Negro, there results from his children and their mixture a
class of individuals who not only are offensive to public view,
blacken communities, modify customs and become intolerable
and burdensome to society; but also being neither Indians nor
Spaniards, they neither maintain docility and dedication to the
agricultural activity of Indians, nor can they be admitted to
the ordinary employments of the others, and thereby they
are useless and prejudicial."

J. M. Quiróz, "Exposición . . . sobre el
comercio de Negros. . . ." 1807

The conquest, occupation, and administration of America
permitted west Europeans from the Iberian peninsula to
construct a society of superiors and inferiors, of lords and
masses, of free and unfree, of taxed and untaxed of Whites
and non-Whites. In the initial stages of culture contact in
heavily populated and advanced culture areas of Mexico and
the Central Andes, Spaniards recognized Amerindian structures of power and status as comparable to their own. They
incorporated elements of the Amerindian elite at the apex of
their native states as well as at the local level. The Amerindian priesthood was ruthlessly obliterated by a conquering
society one of whose dominant preoccupations was outward
religious conformity. Because the Amerindian nobility co-
operated with the Spanish colonialists, they were preserved

to exact tribute and labor from the indigenous masses. They facilitated the Spaniard's system of indirect rule. Spaniards (*peninsulares*) and Whites born in America (*criollos*) concentrated in the large commercial, administrative, and financial centers of the colonial world such as Mexico and Lima, and in the major mining towns. The countryside belonged to the Amerindian population among whom were scattered the Whites on their landed estates or in small towns. In Portuguese America Whites were concentrated in a few port towns such as Recife, Bahia, and Rio de Janeiro; the Brazilian countryside held a small number of nomadic Amerinds, Negroes on plantations, and a sprinkling of White masters. In sum, west European Whites were a tiny minority among millions of people of color. More important for the later social history of Latin America, between the White elite and the mass of Amerinds and Negroes there existed by 1700 a thin stratum of population subject neither to Negro slavery nor Amerindian tutelage, consisting of the products of racial interbreeding among Whites, Amerinds, and Negroes and defined as mestizos, mulattoes, and zambos (mixture of Indian and Negro), and their many combinations.

Miscegenation in America, as elsewhere under the impact and in the aftermath of conquest, was inevitable. In the history of western Europe to 1500, successive waves of incoming migrants had fused with conquered peoples without appreciable, long-term racial discrimination. And when after 1500 west Europeans developed positions in India, for example, their numbers were few, miscegenation was limited, and west Europeans' residence was of short duration. Moreover, a dense East Indian population engulfed both west Europeans and the offspring of west European-East

Indian miscegenation. In contrast, miscegenation in America produced a social stratum which became numerically significant, occupationally required, but in both practice and theory the object of discrimination by the White or near-White elite. To create, then, a two-class or two-stratum society comparable with the Iberian model, the Whites relied on racism not only to keep in their place the Amerinds they found and the Negroes they imported, but also to contain the mestizo, the mulatto, and the castas.

At the outset, however, not only was miscegenation inevitable, it was encouraged. The first factor of miscegenation was the relative absence of west European women in the migratory currents to the new continent; the proportion of male to female immigrants in the colonial period may have approached nine to one. In the sixteenth century in areas of immediate occupation with limitless possibilities of Amerindian labor, tribute and land, the Spaniards frequently married the daughters of the Amerindian nobility, a policy favored by the government to facilitate pacification. Contact was greatest in the major capital cities and mining towns; it was least in the countryside. Once it became impossible for Spanish authorities to control the number or quality of immigrants, west Europeans in America soon overflowed the White men's towns to live parasitically on the Amerindian communities and to take their women as wives. Aside from the element of force often employed, Amerindian women soon learned that their children by Europeans might not be considered Indian, and hence would be subject neither to labor drafts, Indian tribute, nor the many prohibitions which west European masters imposed upon the dependent population.

Furthermore, the west Europeans soon introduced a third

racial factor into the New World melting pot, the African Negro. In Spanish America during the sixteenth and seventeenth centuries, their numbers were limited; most were concentrated in the sugar and tobacco plantations of the Brazilian coast. In Mexico and Peru, Negroes worked in mines or as domestics. And since—as was the case with the west European Whites—the number of Negro women was proportionately low, Negroes found mates among the Amerindian population in urban centers. Negroes soon recognized too that their children by Amerindian women who were, after all, free vassals of the Crown, were also free. Finally, there was frequent intermarriage among mestizos and mulattoes.

It took only a few decades of interracial contact in the New World for the problem of the mestizo, mulatto, and zambo to become evident. Uncontrolled miscegenation complicated the creation of a two-class society where easily recognized phenotype differentiated legal and social status. European Spaniards and criollos constituted the White elite; Amerinds in their communities who were recognizable by language, dress, and food as well as by phenotype, and Negro plantation slaves represented clearly defined groups of tribute-payers or chattels. Racial mixtures, on the other hand, often moved away from either the Indian community or the plantation; they became artisans, wage laborers, or—when employment was limited—vagabonds or vagrants, often preying upon Amerindian communities. Accepted by neither Whites nor Amerinds, obviously unwilling to be chattel slaves, mixed bloods had to survive by developing aggressiveness, ruthlessness, and guile. No wonder that the European and criollo elite soon ascribed not only the assumption of illegitimacy to mestizo and mulatto, but also those charac-

teristics that the dominant people have always ascribed to
the troublesome dominated: a propensity for drunkenness,
promiscuity, and effrontery; a congenital proclivity for rob-
bery and aggression; and a congenital incapacity to abide
by law and order. At the end of the sixteenth century, the
possibility of mestizo-led Indian uprisings, or mulatto-led
slave revolts, produced legislation aimed at curbing their
social incorporation.

If miscegenation was inevitable, it was not inevitable that
the products of miscegenation would come to occupy significant positions in societies differentiated by color and physiognomy. Two developments, however, changed the role of
these interstitial or marginal individuals and magnified their
role in colonial society. First of all, the special conditions of
economic development in the New World, in which Whites
or near-Whites constituted the entrepreneurial class manipulating Amerindian or Negro labor, demanded the presence
of skilled agricultural and mining foremen, cowpunchers,
muledrivers, weavers and blacksmiths, petty merchants and
peddlers. Only freemen of inferior status could and did fill
these occupations. Far better than the Amerindian peoples
with their strong pre-conquest tradition of communal economy and their growing post-conquest dread of the pressures
of the White man's society and economy, the mixed bloods
or castas were integrated into the capitalistic and individualistic world of the White man. As their color "whitened," as
they became less Afro- or Indo-mestizo and more Euro-
mestizo, they occasionally passed upward into the elite
group. In fact, the European's recognition of the possibility
of "stain" of Indian or Negro blood in the American-born
White or criollo furnished a justification for ranking him as
a slightly second-class member of the elite.

Of greater significance in the emergence of the mixed people or castas as a key element of Latin American colonial society was the demographic hecatomb that west Europeans triggered when they came into contact with the Amerindian population and transmitted epidemic disease—smallpox, measles, typhus, especially smallpox—to people lacking immunity. The population became stabilized only in the first half of the seventeenth century. While there is still reluctance to accept recent estimates of New World population on the eve of the conquest, there is no doubt that the decline of Amerindian population by 1600 was staggering. Some claim that the depopulation ratio—the ratio of pre-conquest population to that of about 1650—was on the magnitude of twenty to one, perhaps more. A declining Amerindian element increased the importance of castas in total population as of about 1650; thereafter the slow recovery of Amerindian population and the inflow of west Europeans who mixed with castas gave that group a larger percentage of total population. One is lead inescapably to the conclusion that culture shock, pandemic diseases on a continental basis, and random sexual activity among White west Europeans, native peoples, and forced African immigrants in the sixteenth century opened the way to a new society of vast racial mixture. Racial heterogeneity was already a component of the Latin American colonial heritage. In 1700, to be sure, the castas were still a small percentage of the population in Indo-America as were the mulattoes of Brazil. A very rough distribution suggests they constituted about 6 per cent, the White or near-White about the same, Indian and Negro dependents the rest (88 per cent). Yet the castas were being incorporated functionally in colonial society and economy. In some cases they were already the lowest fringe of the west

European elite. In effect they already showed that they could be co-opted by the elite on the elite's terms by assisting in the exploitation of the masses. Their presence, however, indicates that Iberian colonial society was in fact not a replica of Iberian society.

It was probably in the seventeenth century that the large landowner emerged in America as the dominant figure of both the colonial society and economy. Landowners (and miners) appeared as quasi-seigneurs, with their own chaplains, their own jails, their own stocks and whips for the deviants under their control, their own police forces. Yet the New World seigneurs also provided their own form of security for the obedient: subsistence, protection, and social stability.

The depression of the seventeenth century, the restriction of overseas trade, the near-collapse of metropolitan control, the infrequency of ship sailings, all seem to have shifted social and political power from metropolis to periphery—to the colonial hacendado, mineowner, merchant. At the same time, the compartmentalization of colonial regions was enhanced. Local colonial elites became concerned with their properties, their sub-regions, their provinces. The very colonial commercial system emphasized isolation and compartmentalization. Sectionalism, regionalism, provincialism —whatever it is called, undoubtedly helped produce among Spaniards born in America an incipient nationalism, an ill-defined sense of greater right to rule in America than that enjoyed by European-born administrators and merchants. This early nationalism should not be exaggerated, yet it is evident that there already existed a cleavage within the colonial elite between Americans and Europeans. Europeans considered themselves representatives of the metropolitan power with natural right to control the highest administrative offices, civil, military, and ecclesiastic. And they considered the American-born elite to be inferior, especially since they were aware of the racially mixed background of many of the Americans. Europeans, too, knew the criollos preferred to marry their well-endowed daughters to supposedly racially pure Europeans, rather than to the sons of the American elite who were often spoiled profligates, illustrating the aphorism "Father-merchant, Son-gentleman, Grandson-beggar." But as long as sharp economic divergences failed to develop, the antagonism between criollo and peninsulars remained latent.

3

"Those who leave these kingdoms [of Spain] appointed to colonial posts have against them the presumption that they are usually grasping folk because they move so far from their birthplace to a promised land well suited to wheeling and dealing; and at the time of the judicial review of their conduct, [it becomes clear that] their gains pay for their travel expenses. The evil compounded becomes rapacity. . . . They have no respect for the Audiencias and enjoy complete liberty of action; this is improper because they scarcely administer justice, even less when such governors are related to, or dependents of, a minister of the Council of the Indies whose authority stays the hands of the judges of lower courts since everyone requires and depends upon those who serve Your Majesty on the Council. . . . Your Majesty's court is filled with manipulators who, rejected by Viceroys and Audiencias in the Indies because they are disreputable and incapable of serving Your Majesty, come to Spain without justification to

arrange for themselves the choicest positions, by cunning, underhanded deals and false virtue."

"Consulta del Consejo de las Indias," 1607

"Justice is sold like goods in a market-place where he who has money in his pocket buys what he wants. In this marketplace mystery and secrecy rule. . . . Furthermore, judgments are revealed before they are signed, and interested parties are prepared to elude them or to prevent appeals by the injured. . . . Such justice is like a worm consuming the wealth of the Kingdom."

Viceroy of Mexico, Duque de Linares,
to his successor, 1716

Probably the most salient and enduring feature of any colonial regime, one of the first to appear and the last to leave, is the administrator, the colonial bureaucrat high, middle, and low. He symbolizes the overseas power, the metropolitan authority; he maintains communication, applies the law of the conqueror and adapts local custom and practice to the new colonial requirements, facilitates the consolidation or aggregation of interest groups and their legitimization, provides metropolitan bureaus with information for decision-making, collects taxes. In sum he utilizes the coercive power of the state to preserve the colonial system. He is the palpable representative of the colonial establishment. Without his reports, recommendations, and decisions carefully reproduced in duplicate or triplicate or quadruplicate it would be impossible to write the history of colonial areas. Historians have repaid their debt to the colonial bureaucrat of the Spanish and Portuguese empires in America by their attention, perhaps disproportionate, to the details and processes of colonial administration.

Colonial administration, like any state administrative apparatus, provides a highly visible structure of command and a framework which encloses the more formless processes of social, economic, and cultural change. Its activities require a theory of empire often not explicit, a definition of norms of acceptable behavior and techniques of executing decisions. Inseparable from colonial administration are law codes often expressive of the society's aspirations toward equity and humanitarianism. The combination of formal structures of command and the legal foundations of the colonial state may, however, delude the historian into creating a *myth* in which the colonial structures of personnel recruitment, promotion, review, and retirement, maintained decade after decade and century after century, suggest an independent state service operating judiciously within a visible chain of command along timeless principles of justice evenly administered. This, in brief, has often been the conclusion of historical studies of the Spanish colonial administration in America. We now perceive that bureaucratic *reality* was something else, that the Iberian colonial administrative apparatus constituted a structure for the interweaving of private interest and state goals for the legitimization of conquest and colonization; it served to maintain an exploitative colonial system which liberally sanctioned force whenever necessary. One must never overlook what Iberians in America never forgot: that they occupied the continent by force of arms, by the *derecho de conquista*.

Conquest permitted the government of one of the Spains, Castile, to forge administrative units—the kingdoms or viceroyalties in America such as Mexico and Peru—in theory directly subordinate to the distant kingdom of Castile. Thus Castile created a structure of governance in America lacking late medieval or traditional impediments to pan-regional

operations, e.g. municipal charters allowing independent
decision-making, regional representative bodies or *cortes* incorporating nobility, clergy, and towns, or regional customs
and law. Within the patrimonial state which was the Spanish monarchy, the American colonies were entirely subordinate to the decisions of the monarch and his councils.
Checks and balances had no traditional place within the
colonial system. In this sense the Castilian government theoretically operated with a *tabula rasa* in administrative and
other matters in the colonies. By the same token Castilian
authority in the American kingdoms or viceroyalties was in
theory boundless; only royal representatives could be discretionary and despotic, as abused colonials came to argue in
the eighteenth century.

In practice, the colonial administration, from the ministers
of the Council of the Indies and the Board of Trade in the
metropolis to the viceroys, the judges of the viceregal courts
(*audiencias*), and the local administrators such as corregidores and their subordinates in the so-called Indian "republics," was a vast system of patronage in which peninsulares
and criollos participated.

In the first seventy-odd years of the sixteenth century the
colonization and administration of America was left largely
to individual Iberian entrepreneurs vested with broad powers for *ad hoc* decisions. Conquest situations and undepend-
able communications made effective centralized control impossible. Governmental control was nominal, private interest
paramount. The Spaniards defeated the Amerindian opposition in effect with military bands recruited and financed
with promises of booty and they were expected to maintain
their armed retainers in case of uprisings. They maintained
discipline, accorded civil and criminal justice, and distrib-

uted the dividends of enterprise-as-conquest: the assignment
of native labor in encomienda for estates, mines, and public
works, the disposition of tribute and services owed by the
new Amerindian vassals incorporated or in process of incorporation into the new order. At the local level, the colonial
conquerors, transformed rapidly into mine operators, large-
scale agricultural proprietors, and cattle ranchers, consolidated their position in the town councils whose members
they chose. They were the local aristocracy no matter what
their metropolitan social origins; they were the lords of the
new colonial areas and the first viceroys of Mexico and Peru
between 1535 and about 1550 had to treat them with cir-
cumspection.

From the 1570's onward it was evident that the operations
of private enterprise and colonial administration would have
to be modified to curb the unrestrained ruthlessness of Spaniards and their allies, the *caciques* or Amerindian nobility
through whom they operated to obtain tribute and labor.
For the efficient preservation, organization, and manipulation of Indian communities it was necessary to urbanize,
Christianize, and incorporate them into the west European
economy. Such a solution had to be imposed upon Spanish
entrepreneurs in their long-term interest and in the interests
of a metropolitan government whose resources at home and
in the colonies were already inadequate for imperial grandeur in western Europe. In this process two major interests,
colonial and metropolitan, dovetailed. If the interests of colonial administration demanded that bureaucrats at all levels
curb the sometimes threatening activity of unruly conquerors,
colonial office-holding at the same time furnished opportunities to Spaniards of all ranks and income for employment
and enrichment denied them by the contracting metropolitan

economy. Moreover, the augmented colonial administrative tables of organization gave the Spanish monarchy the chance to sell colonial offices to eager placemen who in turn found other Spaniards ready to advance loans to newly appointed administrators bound for their positions of control over submissive Amerindian masses. So in the last quarter of the sixteenth century conquest turned into pacification with the disappearance of the conquerors and the creation of a colonial bureaucratic superstructure in the areas of the densest Amerindian population—fortuitously those where the most productive silver and gold mines were discovered between 1545 and 1565.

The viceroy, representative of the omnipotent but distant monarch, was entrusted with ultimate responsibility for administering the overseas dependencies of Castile, for harmonizing and balancing interest groups, for preserving colonial hegemony. To positions of such key importance the monarchy appointed figures selected from those whom Spanish society judged fittest by nature to rule—the upper nobility, frequently the grandees. In theory omnipotent, in practice viceregal authority was somewhat fictitious. It was hedged about by countervailing forces: the audiencia, judicial review of the viceroy's performance at the end of his tenure (*residencia*), and the influence of corporative bodies with special jurisdiction, such as the ecclesiastical establishment and the merchant guild whose interests a viceroy could not lightly override however respectful the tone in which their demands were phrased. Furthermore, because the tenure of viceroys was brief, from roughly three to five or more years, they were obliged to rely upon the secretariat of the viceroyalty for the flow of information, assessment, advice. Like the kings in Spain, viceroys always ran the risk of be-

coming the instruments rather than the masters of their ad-
visers.

During the late sixteenth century these chief colonial officers seem to have generally dominated the local interests,
even to have imposed decisions upon powerful interest
groups established overseas—encomenderos, estate-owners,
merchants, regular and secular churchmen. In the next century the contraction of the Spanish economy and the conse-
quent slackening of imperial power and control were mirrored in the quality of colonial administrators. Whereas in
the sixteenth century viceroys were capable grandees, in the
seventeenth the grandees sought colonial service for the opportunity to create fortunes for themselves, the members of
their extended families, and their clients. Instead of imposing solutions, one senses that they strove for consensus
among conflicting groups on the basis of bribery not of
equity. In this fashion powerful colonial interests in effect
manipulated viceroys who found in colonial office economic
opportunities lacking in the metropolis. By 1700 the major
problem in the colonial administration was how to disen-
gage viceroys from quick absorption by colonial vested interests with influential friends at court and ample expense
accounts.

Below the viceroy probably the most influential institution
of the viceroyalty was the viceregal court or audiencia, sometimes a check upon his discretionary powers, often his substitute in case of death. Unlike its metropolitan counterpart, it
was empowered with broad judicial and administrative
functions. Its judges or oidores who provided basic continuity and the preservation of imperial over regional interests
were invariably lawyers (*letrados*) appointed from among
the alumni of the great metropolitan law schools (*colegios*

mayores). They were often shifted among colonial audiencias, then recalled to complete service in the metropolis and to enjoy the returns of colonial service: colonial investments, pensions, annuities. Like the viceregal secretariat, the *fiscales* or crown attorneys of the audiencia furnished legal advice on the wide spectrum of matters brought to the attention of the viceroy. Yet they too, no matter what the constraints placed upon their involvement, were enmeshed in local interests. The town councils (*cabildos*), controlled by the criollo elite, were limited to town administration.

In theory this administrative infra- and superstructure was subordinated to one of the councils in Spain, the Council of the Indies, many of whose members often had served on audiencias in the colonies. This contact and experience permitted them to act in Spain as representatives of colonial groups seeking to circumvent innovation detrimental to their interests.

During the period of administrative consolidation in the seventeenth century little innovation appeared. The quality of office-holders probably declined due principally to the increasing sale of public office in Spain and the empire. Venality and corruption became generalized, institutionalized, and legitimized as employment in the colonial bureaucracy became a major source of status and income for the Spanish aristocracy and gentry, their extended circles of relatives, clients, and dependents, and for the sons of the middle class who were able to attend the metropolitan law schools. The interaction of legally sanctioned monopoly and of private interest inevitably produced an atmosphere in which corruption was tolerated and aggressive individualism was concealed or disguised by the apparent functional corporative nature of society. In the context of a society based upon scholastic natural law, liberty was exercised within the corporative body. Those involved in the administration of the colonies found its principles and practice anything but oppressive. And where colonial legislation conflicted with local interest, it could always be suspended or ignored as suggested by the often utilized formula "to be obeyed but not executed."

Early in the conquest colonial administration received ecclesiastical authority when the papacy conferred upon the Castilian monarchy full supervision over the ecclesiastical establishment—appointment, administration, revenue collection—in return for conversion of Amerinds and maintenance of the church. Two centuries after the conquest and the initial challenge of evangelism and social engineering among Amerinds stripped of their religious leaders and symbols, the Roman Catholic church represented the faith of the conqueror and his state at all levels of society. Archbishop to curate, the human representatives of the church were Whites although by 1700 mestizos were beginning to appear at the parish level. Gone were the earlier days of evangelistic experimentation with Amerindian culture to forge a society without oppression and misery, a society of Christian communitarians molded in the spirit of More's *Utopia*. Gone were the pioneer and exhilarating days of experiments in education for the sons of the Amerindian nobility. The demands of both metropolitan and colonial society and economy required the church to abandon its crusading and reformist zeal; by 1700 the main body of Christian evangelists had been removed to the frontiers in America —northern Mexico, the upper Amazon, the upper La Plata basin—to serve as buffer between Amerindian nomads and colonial settlements.

Within Spanish America the curate functioned beside the

corregidor or alcalde mayor. Almost invariably a Spaniard
or criollo, supported by tithes and religious fees, he administered to the Amerinds the sacraments allowed them,
and mediated between the cosmos and the Amerindian
world by legitimizing hierarchy, subordination, control.
What is today termed social overhead—schools, hospitals,
charity—the ecclesiastical establishment financed and administered. At the local level these services encouraged abiding loyalty to the state and the faith of the parishioners.

But the ecclesiastical establishment's function was more
extensive than this. By 1700 contributions of the faithful and
intelligent financial policies had made the wealth and income of the colonial church as proverbial in the colonies as
in the metropolises. Pious endowments in convents, monas-
teries, and major churches supplied investment funds to
miners, merchants, landowners. The legacies confided to
them represented investment to ensure income for the heirs
of families of substance who had entered the church. From
church funds in America flowed income to maintain ecclesiastical offices and establishments in Spain and Portugal and
ultimately Rome itself. In return, colonial churchmen, high,
middle, and low, contributed to the stability of the colonial
state and society by exhorting parishioners to fidelity to the
monarchy and to its local representatives. Treason against
the state was equated with heresy, as the edicts of the church
were to argue in the wars of independence. In brief, the
interpenetration of church and state, so significant a political
feature of the politics of Latin America in the nineteenth
century, was born in the sixteenth and fully developed by
1700.

As historians have moved beyond political history to economic and social history, they have learned that examina-

tion of institutions and practices utilized by an elite and applied to the masses at the local level—for example, debt peonage in India's Bihar province, *pongaje* or obligatory domestic service by Indians in highland Peru, or sharecropping and the welfare system in Mississippi delta counties— reveals the operation of a political system far more nakedly than, for instance, an examination of the structure of judicial appeal. The same may be said for the corregimiento or alcaldía mayor in Spain's colonial centers in Peru and Mexico.

The face of Iberian colonialism, of conquest, pacification, and evangelization may be seen in the basic administrative unit of Central Mexico and highland Peru of 1700, the corregimiento. There would be found the corregidor de indios or alcalde mayor, a literate Spaniard of generally limited legal training who had obtained appointment by purchase, family connection, or patronage. Since there was no regular promotional system at this bureaucratic level and salaries were low, the corregidor assumed his isolated post to maximize his one- to five-year tenure to accumulate a fortune. Moreover, the corregidor or alcalde mayor had undoubtedly borrowed from merchants at Madrid, Sevilla, Mexico, or Lima to cover outlays on bribes, on the tax of one-half the first year's salary (*media anata*), and on clothing, household goods, and travel. On arrival at his post, the corregidor was already integrated into an administrative, financial, and mercantile system whose infrastructure consisted of the Amerindian vassal, half-serf and half-peasant, and whose superstructure might be represented by an affluent ex-viceroy ensconced in his Madrid townhouse with dozens of retainers.

In the Central Andes a corregidor's major responsibility

as district chief was to exact from caciques in Amerindian towns the annual quota of draftees for silver and mercury mines—in particular the dreaded mita de Potosí. Enforcement of the labor draft offered corregidores ample opportunity to accept bribes from Indians seeking to escape mine service or from estate owners and sweatshop entrepreneurs seeking extra hands. Yet the most efficient way for such a corregidor to amass a fortune was via unsanctioned but hallowed practice of forcing Amerinds to accept goods—wanted or unwanted, from mules to mercery—whose quantities and prices he prescribed. The colonial district chief or corregidor handled goods sent by merchants in the viceregal capital, more than likely connected with Sevilla exporters who had originally financed the corregidor's purchase of office. In essence this was an important facet of the system of trade and navigation between Spain and the Indies.

To the corregidor, miner, and merchant must be added another representative of the colonial establishment, the parish priest in the *corregimiento de indios*. Acquiring his position in the devious manner of secular placemen, his obligations were often taken lightly. The curate had his commercial "rights" too: "gifts" of food and clothing, religious fees, unremunerated household service. This, of course, is not a comprehensive catalogue of the instruments of bureaucratic extortion in Indian America around 1700: it is only to suggest the secular roots of Amerindian fear of the European and the criollo and their mestizo, mulatto, or cacique assistants.

These intimations of brutal exploitation of Amerindian masses may seem unduly exaggerated. They have not been presented to indict a people but a system. Obviously, only a minority of Iberians profited from the overseas possessions while the mass of Iberians remained oblivious or powerlessly aware of colonial oppression. Nor is it intended to overlook the fact that sensitive Spaniards and Portuguese often denounced exploitation and inhumanity perpetrated by their fellow Europeans in the American colonies. If the condition of the lowest stratum of society in Spanish colonial America was generally wretched, some will insist that the existence of west European peasants, craftsmen, and miners in the sixteenth and seventeenth centuries was equally wretched. This proposition in general is valid, and the difficulties inherent in calculating relative deprivation make criticism difficult unless one probes a bit further.

Were west Europeans forced into mines and kept there in the seventeenth century without surfacing from Monday to Saturday? Was there in operation in western Europe an annual labor draft which forced unwilling laborers to move hundreds of miles to pitheads along with their families, supplies, and pack animals? To change the scene, were there west European occupations in which employers could calculate with frightening accuracy that a worker's life would be no longer than five to ten years in their employment—which the Brazilian planters calculated for Negro slaves on sugar plantations in the first half of the seventeenth century? Or, not to exhaust comparisons but to show their possibilities, could a high west European official have returned from a post after four years of service with an income surplus of between 1 and 1.5 million silver pesos? For example, the Duque de Alburquerque in 1715 paid the Madrid government 700,000 silver pesos to avoid charges of gross malfeasance in office. If the answer to these questions is no, then the historian no matter how insensitive his skin must conclude that west Europeans from the Iberian peninsula utilized the right of conquest to exploit the subordinate peoples of America for personal profit beyond possibilities existing in the metropolis. Colonialism and uplift have always been antithetical.

A civil service invariably mirrors the matrix, metropolitan or colonial, in which it operates. By the end of the seventeenth century, the Spanish and Spanish colonial civil service reflected societies they were designed to administer. The rigidity of Spanish society, the inability or unwillingness to reshape the economy, the stagnation of Spain gave the elite and their wide circle of dependents by birth, marriage, or service few opportunities for employment other than in state service in the metropolis and especially in the colonies. To the colonies flowed a succession of viceroys chosen from the upper nobility and given wide discretion for enrichment. There they administered submissive colonial peoples in conjunction with the colonial audiencias. Beneath viceroys and audiencias came large numbers of Spanish placemen who had purchased preferment, indebted themselves to Spanish moneylenders, and who then proceeded to enrich themselves as corregidores or alcaldes mayores or their lieutenants in isolated Amerindian communities.

Thus by about 1700 the characteristic features of the colonial policy were already well established. Public office at all levels was seen as a legitimate instrument to further private interest over public weal. A monarchy extorting a share of a viceroy's spoils of office symbolized, indeed legitimized, venality, encouraged corruption and showed itself demonstrably incapable of controlling malfeasance in office. It is an ironic commentary on the effects of colonial rule that the very term "cacique"—originally applied to Amerinds who served the colonial elite to exploit the Amerindian masses—

was to become in Spain the term for a local boss. Furthermore, the local colonial government of town officials, corregidores, and priests emerged as the core of political power that fused the interests of local elite of wealth, power, and prestige. It was expected that the colonial civil service armed with broad discretionary powers would work closely with local interests to enforce the *status quo* by manipulating the colonial law code. To the elite, law became a norm honored in the breach. To the unprivileged, law was arbitrary and alien, therefore without moral force.

PART TWO

1700–1810

CHAPTER IV

The Eighteenth Century

"Spain, although so well situated as to open to her citizens the most opulent trade, is so deteriorated that she enjoys the title of ownership rather than the utility of what is produced."
"Ordenanzas nuevas . . . para el comercio y
trafico de las Indias. . . ." 1708

"The world's trade flourishes at the expense of the peoples of America and their immense labors, but the riches they draw from the bosom of the fertile earth are not retained."
Memoir to the Viceroy of Mexico, 1723

By 1700 the American colonies and their Iberian metropolises were closely linked in a relationship that was far more essential to the metropolises than to their colonial dependencies. More important, however, the link had become critically weakened by the breakdown of imperial economic and administrative controls. Portugal resolved this crisis by acknowledging its role of economic dependent upon England in exchange for the security of empire. Spain remained unwilling to accept tutelage for security, for influential Spaniards had come to believe that empire in America still contained possibilities for national recovery through the restoration of control and economic growth in the colonies.

The generalized crisis of Spain at the death of Charles II and the following thirteen years of internal and international war terminated in a semblance of stabilization—one might call it the stabilization of exhaustion—in the Treaty of Utrecht. Under that treaty's terms Spain, stripped of its vestigial European dependencies and the possession of Gibraltar, was guaranteed possession of the empire in America. Practical recognition of colonial control was achieved by conceding economic privileges to the English: the supply of slaves (*asiento*) and the direct sale of a stipulated volume of goods. To the French was conceded access to the colonial economy by tacit toleration of French merchants in Spain and the prospect of economic and political co-operation against the English.

From the crucible of war and the Utrecht settlement emerged the basis of Spain's eighteenth-century colonial policy, often obscured by procrastination, withdrawal, and frequent compromise of substance. As a whole the policy was one of economic "nationalization" of the domestic and colonial economies. The implementation of policy required, first, recovery of the commercial concessions yielded to European nations in the last half of the seventeenth century, confirmed and—in the case of the English—expanded by Utrecht: termination of the asiento and the direct introduction of goods, and the elimination of contraband channels at Gibraltar, Cadiz, and the colonies. Next, to meet European pressures in the form of demand for the colonies' silver, foodstuffs, and raw materials, and for their use as outlets for manufactures, the Spanish government began to tap neglected colonial economies, for example, those of Buenos Aires, Caracas, and Havana. Third, to meet domestic and colonial import requirements, the policy envisaged fomenting metropolitan agriculture and manufacture. Thus, economic autonomy would develop by maximizing the colonial compact. Finally, essential to the policy was "recovery" of control of the Andalusian entrepôt of all colonial trade flows, "nationalizing" its entrepreneurs by facilitating the transformation of Spaniards at Cadiz from factors or agents of foreign firms supplying capital, goods, and insurance into independent merchants; this implied ultimate withdrawal of influential French and English merchant firms established there.

Implementation of this proto-economic nationalism was advanced gradually to reinvigorate existing structures of polity, economy, society. The interlocked network of entrenched domestic and international interest permitted no other goal in an underdeveloped nation whose elite did not call into question the inherent soundness, the viability of the tradition of monarchy, aristocracy, and privilege. The policy and its methods of implementation fit best the general term of "restoration" as it was then conceived or, as it would be categorized today, "defensive overhaul" or "defensive modernization." But, by no means was this the product of a "bourgeois revolution" in Spain.

2

"War sometimes becomes necessary for the support of trade, and therefore the wisdom of a nation does not so much consist in preserving peace, as in choosing the proper opportunity for enjoying war. . . ."

A Supplement to Britain's Mistakes in the
Commencement and Conduct of the
Present War. . . . 1740

"All the energy of the Junta has been directed toward smoothing paths and obstacles so that Spaniards may again become

true merchants as were formerly their ancestors, by closing the
channels whereby Foreigners have acquired the despotic con-
trol of trade and navigation that oppresses and will ruin us
if not blocked."

E. Larruga, "Historia de la real y general
junta de comercio, moneda y minas. . . ,"
about 1780

It was the purpose of French Bourbon policy to make Spain
and its colonies effective allies in the development of the
French economy and in the conflict with England. This
policy was bound to clash with the complex web of interests
created under the Hapsburgs. First and foremost was one of
the most influential economic groups after 1700, the mercantile oligopolists of Cadiz who were agents of foreign interests in most cases. They were tied by interest and family, by
status and ideology to the colonial commercial centers at
Veracruz and Mexico City, at Lima and Manila, and by
common interest in political action to the Andalusian
grandee-landlords. Given the compartmentalization of
Spain, its largely agrarian economy, its exports of raw materials, and above all its dependence upon the colonies, the
Cadiz merchants in their consulado or guild commanded
Spain's leading sector, its colonial trade. The manipulation
of colonial interests, mercantile, bureaucratic, fiscal, and ec-
clesiastic, all centered on Cadiz after the eclipse of Sevilla.
As a bloc they were a bulwark of the *status quo* which the
French civil servants and their Spanish counterparts under
Philip V wished to revamp.

Before the War of the Spanish Succession, Madrid policy-
makers whether concerned with foreign policy or economic
policy were preoccupied with the fate of the colonies in
America. It was understood that the Bourbons and their ad-

ministrators trained under Colbert might undertake reforms in Spain's domestic economy and in colonial trade—issues on which the Spanish elite remained divided throughout the eighteenth century. One may hypothesize that the essence of Spanish Bourbon economic policy was the abandonment of "passive" trade for what is today economic nationalism via import-substitution, that is, via protection. This was a policy of reform and renovation. In order of priority there came first the creation of a new corps of administrators, better trained, indoctrinated in the idea of service to the state rather than the locality or the region, whose performance at home and in the colonies might improve the quality of leadership. This was followed by the elimination of commercial privileges that Spain had to grant England at Utrecht and which gave English interests legitimate access to the empire: the right to introduce at Veracruz, Havana, Cartagena, and Buenos Aires both an annual number of African slaves and a quantity of manufactures—both privileges the source of contraband on an uncontrollable scale. Third, the new policy-makers recognized they must increase the flow of goods from Cadiz to the artificially undersupplied colonies.

These policy intentions affecting Spain's colonial world were only part of the spectrum of change contemplated by the Bourbon-inspired administrators employed by Philip V's government. The traditional view of Bourbon Spain is to emphasize the "reform" surge in the metropolis. The impulsions of change or adjustment were linked, but if priority must be assigned, then the colonial stimuli must be ranked first. For the economic growth of eighteenth-century Spain was predicated upon the immediate and long-term possibilities of the colonial economy as the eighteenth-century political economists or *proyectistas* from Ustariz and Campillo to Ulloa and Ward insisted.

The dismal literature on Spain's economic backwardness did produce a spirit of inquiry and experimentation toward the end of the seventeenth century notably in the formation of the Junta de Comercio. Undoubtedly the internal schism of the Spanish regional elites at the death of Charles II reflected two major groups or factions—one hesitates to call them parties. One sought to preserve structures linking metropolis and colonies in a web of backwardness; the other believed in strengthening them further and in turning to Spain's greater benefit the exploitation of the American possessions. This latter group looked to the initiative of France and its representatives in Spain under Philip for analysis and implementation of change directed from the top. To the Spanish elite who questioned the viability and utility of some traditional practices, the new bureaucrats symbolized change within the structures of the past. Aristocracy would be subordinated but, what was most important, preserved. And both conservative and realistic elite members agreed on the basic principle that aristocratic distinctions were to be maintained.

The modifications undertaken or contemplated for metropolitan Spain suggest the goal of unification, political as well as economic. Peripheral was to be joined to central Spain. Catalonia, stripped of many regional rights, and Aragon were incorporated and Catalonia at last began to trade with America via the Andalusian port of Cadiz. The attempt to incorporate the Basque provinces failed because Basque privileges sheltered an intricate web of institutions and practices. These included not only the important commercial houses of Bilbao, which would accept incorporation only in return

for equal and direct access to the empire comparable with
that of Cadiz, but also capillaries of contraband leading to
the Castilian and Aragonese frontiers. Further to erode regional enclaves, the French-inspired system of royal inten-
dants armed with broad fiscal and military powers was
introduced not only to rationalize tax collection but also to
reduce barriers to interregional trade, viz., transit tolls and
local taxes which virtually immured Cadiz from the entry of
goods produced in Spain and exported to the colonies.
Elimination of such barriers could facilitate the flow to
peripheral Spain's ports of manufactures produced in
another French-inspired institution, government subsidized
factories for production of fine woolens and silks, porcelain
and tapestries. Finally, creation of chartered companies
capped the program for stimulating production for export
via Cadiz to America. The companies, regional corporations
such as the Barcelona, Zaragoza, and Guipuzcoan companies, were granted special sectors of the colonial market to
ensure their success. For only in "protected" markets of the
colonies could the output of Spanish manufactories be distributed at a profit.

What emerges from the proyectistas' diagnoses and blue-
prints and from attempts at domestic change is that neither
political economists nor Bourbon administrators were inno-
vators. They emphasized tradition, caution, and circumspec-
tion. Even some of the mildly critical works, for example,
Campillo's *Nuevo sistema,* had their publication delayed for
decades. This is not to deprecate the refreshing interest of an
enlightened minority in integrating a territory into a nation,
reducing regional, class, and corporate privilege, facilitating
the movement of goods from section to section, raising agricultural productivity via incentives both to estate owners and

semi-feudal peasantry, establishing textile mills, creating a national highway and canal network, and finally increasing the flow of Spanish products to the American colonies. What is striking is the continuity of wishful thinking invariably coupled with prudent retreat made all the more possible by the low visibility of political decision-making. Conflicts of interest before the national and international public were conveniently concealed behind the pragmatic rhetoric of repeated royal pronouncements.

Why, it will be asked, the gap between wishful thinking and prudent retreat? Why the impression of half-hearted, ineffectual, and ephemeral purpose rather than solid achievement—certainly an accurate assessment of Spanish performance until 1763? Political schizophrenia was the product of the realization of the need for adjustment and the fear of affronting vested interests, the ecclesiastical establishment, the landholding nobility, the privileged corporations like the Five Major Guilds of Madrid, or the unholy alliance between Spain's two most influential pressure groups, the Andalusian landlords and Cadiz merchants who tenaciously argued, pressured, bribed, and if necessary threatened in behalf of the preservation of their respective hallowed privileges. "Hallowed privileges" is used advisedly, for the Cadiz merchants in their consulado turned to the distant past for signposts to the present, to the legislation of Charles V and Philip II, to the "sacred laws of the Indies" and its *Recopilación* as their memorials unfailingly noted.

From the second decade of the eighteenth century, when Philip V's administration sanctioned the final shift of the American trade monopoly from Sevilla to Cadiz, the Cadiz merchants in their guild almost invariably seconded by their merchant colleagues in Mexico City and Lima sought to pre-

serve intact a kind of mercantile *mayorazgo,* the inheritance
of almost two centuries of conquest and exploitation of
the American colonies. At the outset, Cadiz lobbied and
schemed against the still renovating but highly insecure first
Bourbon administration, by forcing Philip's administrators
in the 1720's to back down from their attempt to return both
Consulado and Casa de Contratación to Sevilla where contraband operations were more difficult.

The interests of this transatlantic guild, the interlocking
interest in maximum profit-taking by the twenty to thirty
Cadiz wholesale importers, exporters, and shipping magnates, and a slightly smaller but perhaps even more influential number of guild representatives in Mexico City and
Lima, were never lost sight of: control of any and all goods
in the transatlantic trade. The guild merchants of this far-
flung corporation were truly internationalists: they handled
the goods of all Europe, of France, England, Holland, the
Hanse ports and, yes, even of Spain, if price and other conditions were attractive.

If the government in Madrid occasionally balked at trading practices which profited Cadiz merchants and suppliers
while providing no sustained stimulus to the peninsula as a
whole, and criticized their shopkeeper's mentality (*economía
de bodegón*), agents in Madrid representing the interlocking merchants of Cadiz and Mexico quickly offered
loans to an always penurious government, as the Sevillan
monopolists had done in the sixteenth and seventeenth centuries; they also offered bribes to equally penurious bureaucrats. If some misguided but well-intentioned officials prepared position papers somewhat critical of the national
effects of Cadiz's privileges, there were apparently ways of
preventing the publication of their manuscripts, if not for-

ever, then for decades. By serving faithfully their own interest, the Cadiz and related groups asserted they were serving
equally faithfully the interest of the Crown.

The interest groups of Andalusia were the most significant in terms of the extent and depth of involvement in
metropolitan and colonial areas. The complex structure controlled at Cadiz in the eighteenth century extended from
Madrid to the commercial and administrative nuclei in
America and down to the level of corregimiento and alcaldía
mayor. But the structure they dominated and supported
was not their sole monopoly. The web of interlocking interest in the colonies, of civil service, church, and merchants
everywhere and at all levels tended to absorb pressures for
change whether to create higher standards for corregidores,
to insist upon more frequent visits by curates to their parishioners, to demand more regular convoy sailings to supply
America more adequately, or to open all Spain's seaports to
direct trade with the Americas. It was well known that judi-
cious bribes to high government officials could also prevent
discussion of necessary adjustments in administrative and
economic matters, or to block enforcement of change if the
Madrid authorities so ordered for the colonies. On balance,
by the time of the accession of Charles III in 1759 little in the
way of effective change had occurred in the metropolis.
There is no reason to presume that conditions in Spain, a
backward, peripheral, and dependent area of western Europe in the eighteenth century, might have pressured the
Madrid government to modify the colonial administrative or
trading systems. What galvanized Spain to take some action
in America was an external stimulus: the threat to the colonial end of the transatlantic trade pipeline, the pressure of
English merchants operating from the Jamaican base in the

...obean, flooding colonial markets, underselling Spanish-...dled goods, disorganizing the time-honored fleet and fair system, and after 1740 threatening to bypass wholly the Cadiz entrepôt. By about 1750 the Madrid authorities recognized the storm warnings of the aggravating colonial problem. Spanish authorities spent almost fifty years after Utrecht fiddling with changes in the obviously inadequate trading and administrative system. It took them only three years, once the British had seized Havana and Manila simultaneously in 1762 and threatened to attack Veracruz, to begin a series of changes long contemplated and tenaciously resisted by entrenched groups among the Spanish elite at home and in the colonies.

3

[Referring to the possible innovation, that the Spanish government might exclude foreign countries from its trade and navigation, develop industry and capital resources] "The nations of Europe which preserve a certain equilibrium among themselves and are interested that no country expand beyond its limits nor try to conquer any of the Spanish possessions, satisfied with carrying on their trade and dispatching their goods to these kingdoms, in view of such an innovation, would change their system and seek illegal trade with the Spanish Possessions of America arms in hand, perhaps to conquer some or incite others to rebellion, which would force Spain to sustain a burdensome war without allies, for which reasons it is appropriate that Spain prefer ... to foment its trade, navigation and agriculture, remaining satisfied for the moment with protecting cottage industry of linen and wool."

"Observaciones . . . al Marqués de
Sonora. . . ." 1778

"Virtually the whole theory of this modest science [political economy] boils down in our case to eliminating blocks, opening communications and facilitating exports. And yet so great was the emphasis that our system [Spanish commercial policy] placed upon carrying on trade alone and with the door closed, that only once each year, or, later, on permitted occasions, was there opened to other nations the only, narrow little door that its merchants controlled and by handfuls they measured its steps and operations. In such great darkness we spent almost three centuries and during that darkness, neither was there perceived the Metropolis' backwardness and lack of industry, nor the portentous change that time had produced in the world's political and scientific situation."

Francisco Arango y Parreño, *Expediente . . . sobre los medios. . . para sacar la agricultura y comercio de esta Ysla del apuro en que se hallan,* 1808

Loss of Manila and Havana to the English in August 1762 and English control over that city until July of 1763 shocked metropolitan Spaniards and colonial subjects. A fortress-town considered impregnable guarding the route of outbound silver fleets, a possible staging area for attack upon Veracruz and through it to Mexico, Havana was long considered essential to the preservation of Spanish control over America. Its temporary loss was provocative and sobering. Even more thought-provoking was the recognition that before 1762 no more than fifteen ships called there in any single year, while in eleven months of English control, over 700 merchant vessels alone entered with English manufactures, and with foodstuffs, timber, animals, and ironware from Britain's North American colonies, and with slaves.

The rapidity with which some changes were implemented and others contemplated both in America and Spain leads to the conclusion that loss of Havana after what seemed only token resistance triggered pressures building up. The acces-

sion of Charles III in 1759 signaled a deep sea-change. Unlike royal predecessors for generations, Charles had matured
away from the Madrid court, away from the pressures which
seemed to have rendered Spanish kings since Philip II incapable of independent decision-making. As king of Naples,
Charles had picked a corps of capable administrators ready
to tamper with privilege and tradition and embittered by un-
varnished English intervention to maintain Naples subservient to English mercantile interests. Charles came to
Madrid with the intent of reviewing Spanish institutions,
leadership, and performance, and imbued with proto-
economic nationalism. He brought with him Neapolitan
administrators of proven competence and dedication, outstanding among them Esquilache. In Spain, Charles found
too a corps of collaborators among the lower nobility and
the Spanish equivalent of gentry, who had risen from lower
officer rank in the army or who had attended minor univer-
sities to pursue careers in the law. Their distinguishing characteristic was talent, not family name. Since no one in Spain
or anywhere else in Europe of that time could rise without
patronage, the men of talent surrounding Charles had good
connections. They were, in a way, the first generation of
Spanish administrators who on occupying positions of
power were predisposed to assimilate and adapt to Spanish
needs the adjustments to traditional societies then in vogue
in Russia, Prussia, and notably France.

They should not be confused with uncritical imitators for
they were intensely nationalistic yet far from unrealistic
about how far Spanish strata of power and wealth could or
should be pushed to effect changes administrators envisioned. The notorious "popular" urban riot in Madrid and
in other Spanish cities in 1766 ostensibly caused by new reg-

ulations prescribing the cut of capes and proscribing the wide-brimmed hats supposedly dear to Spaniards was—as Charles and Esquilache and their assistants sensed immediately—a warning not to proceed with radical adjustments. Charles, an absolute monarch, fled from Madrid. And the untitled men of talent called to power by the high-born, the titled, and the powerful knew they were to cajole Spanish interest groups to accept only necessary adjustments; they were not appointed to demolish the commanding heights of privilege. Thereafter, Spanish adjustments occurred in the metropolis but slowly and hesitantly. In colonial matters changes may have been pursued with somewhat more intensity but this should not be exaggerated. Nor should efforts under Charles to reduce the role of English interests in Spain and in the colonial empire be considered unique. For beginning in 1755 Pombal in Portugal set in motion chartered companies and administrative reforms for the colony in Brazil and assisted industrial enterprise in the metropolis to supply the colonial market—all aimed precisely at the goal of proto-economic nationalism permitting the execution of policies which English interests in the Iberian peninsula and the Iberian colonies considered inimical. The Iberian satellites of western Europe's more advanced economies had seemingly resolved to pull themselves up by their colonial bootstraps.

One may view the reign of Charles III as the apogee of three centuries of Spanish colonialism in America. Demographic growth, the development of long neglected areas for the production of sugar, cacao, tobacco, and hides, the extraordinary increase in the annual production of Mexico's silver mines, all attracted the attention of England and France and obliged Spaniards to review colonial policies or

see first the colonies' trade wholly captured by west European
competitors, then the colonies themselves. Cautiously the
structure of colonial trade was revamped first in the Caribbean
(1765) when a number of ports in Spain were opened to direct
contact with Caribbean ports without a mandatory call at
Cadiz; next, thirteen Spanish ports were permitted to trade
directly with all major colonial ports (1778) except Veracruz
and La Guayra (Venezuela) which were at last included in
1789. These minor adjustments, publicized as a "free trade"
policy, represented only a liberalization of trade *within* the
imperial framework. Limited intercolonial trade was allowed only in colonial products, for no re-export of European imports was sanctioned. The convoyed fleet system was
gradually abandoned and by 1778 eliminated. The aim of
these changes was to improve contact between metropolis
and colonies, to reduce contraband by increasing supply, and
to raise the percentage of Spanish manufactures in Spain's
trade with the colonies. To Spain's first national bank, the
Banco de San Carlos, was granted a monopoly of silver and
gold transfers to western Europe, to Holland, France, and
England after specie and bullion had arrived at Spanish
ports. By 1789 Spanish administrators took satisfaction in a
significant rise in value and volume of colonial trade, in the
colonial remittances of profits and surpluses, and in what
some considered a noteworthy percentage growth in the
volume of Spanish products from Spanish shops, factories,
and distilleries—woolens, paper, ironware, wines, and brandies. Upsurge in the flow of goods and metals increased
government revenue from customs duties, sales taxes, tobacco and mercury monopolies. Most important, the volume
of silver produced in America and drawn largely from Mexico's Guanajuato mining center rose encouragingly. By 1800
Mexico produced 66 per cent of the world's silver output

and Spain's American colonies contributed 90 per cent of
total world output.

From the unsolicited testimony of private citizens and the
reports of officials sent to review candidly colonial conditions, Madrid bureaucrats under Charles III recognized the
illegal but tolerated mechanisms whereby appreciable colonial income leaked to English, French, and Dutch contra-
banders. It was held that the colonial structures of administration needed subdivision where required, and everywhere
competent, efficient and honest administrators. So new and
more manageable territorial divisions were designed and key
administrators largely drawn from the officer corps ordered
to staff viceregal and other administrative posts. Fear of English aggression against colonial ports was a prime factor,
too, in the appointment of competent military. More important was the belief that the dedication to state service, the
rigors of training and discipline, the standards of honor of
the military insured execution of Madrid's colonial plans
and reduction of administrators' complicity in contraband.
Under Charles members of the nobility received responsibility where they were capable of bearing it. However, at a
moment when the colonial elite groups were growing,
Madrid gave little indication in its policy of colonial appointment that those born in the colonies qualified as execu-
tors of colonial policy.

It follows from the proto-economic nationalism of the Iberian countries in the last half of the eighteenth century that
policy-makers intended full control over their colonies' economy to effect a policy of neutrality in the conflict between
England and France. They recognized that centuries of
colonialism had provided income to the metropolitan elite,
but not domestic productive resources. In the eighteenth century they were as dependent as ever upon the dominant

economies of western Europe. They recognized too that fuller utilization of the colonies' natural and human resources would ensure perpetuation of traditional structures of privilege and power. Spanish administrators turned to France for assistance because the French monarchy, aristocracy, and bourgeoisie shared the same view of society and polity, of inherited privilege, and because Hispano-French collaboration might prevent the English from seizing choice colonial areas in America. To the French such collaboration promised their manufacturers, merchants, and financiers indirect access to the Spanish empire. The Spaniards hoped collaboration would flower into an independent and respected Spain; the French banked on developing Spain for assistance to withstand England and to obtain from Spain and its colonies silver, raw materials for French industry, consumers for its output. The French hoped to keep Spain underdeveloped but contented. To the English, Franco-Spanish collaboration was only further inducement to contraband aggressively via Caribbean possessions and in South America via Rio de Janeiro and southern Brazil into the Rio de la Plata.

Independence, however, was then and is still predicated upon a national economy able to produce in quantity basic capital goods and—in the case of colonial powers of the eighteenth century—to maintain maritime communications at all times. By the outbreak of the French revolution, Pombal's policies had been reversed by his successors, and mining and associated interests in central Brazil had almost engineered rebellion. In Spain, despite the official euphoria realists had few illusions about the potentialities of adjustment. A policy of gradualism in colonial policy had not effectively weakened the dominant role of Cadiz and its allies in oli-

gopoly in Mexico City, in Lima, and in Manila. More than
85 per cent of colonial trade moved through Cadiz where
facilities for shipping, insurance, warehousing, and communication were still superior to those in other Spanish ports.
Oligopolists of Cadiz and their overseas collaborators resisted intercolonial trade, blocked expansion of colonial ship-
building, preferred to deal with their traditional suppliers of
manufactures in England and France or even in Silesia
rather than with the non-competitive Spanish producers. In
a word, they preferred to monopolize the flow of west European goods through Cadiz and resisted the attempt by
Madrid officials to stimulate the economy of peripheral
Spain by providing access to American colonial markets.
The very structure of oligopoly at Cadiz and in the colonies
and the policy of constraints on supply and price served as
inducement to contraband. In Portugal and Spain in the
1780's few policy-makers believed it was possible to match
the economic performance of the English whose shipping
was more efficient, whose insurance rates were lower, whose
inexpensive cotton goods rapidly fired an insatiable demand
in Mediterranean Spain and Portugal and especially in the
Iberian colonies in the tropics and sub-tropics. Spain, Portugal, and their colonies seemed to Iberian realists locked
into a level of economic dependence already centuries old,
and some analysts were drawn to physiocracy and thereby to
rationalize the role of the peninsula and the overseas empires
in America as producers of Europe's silver and gold, sugar,
cacao, tobacco, coffee, hides, dyestuffs, and cotton. The
meager return on Iberian policies of adjustment was perhaps inevitable. By responding only when and where circumstance made change unavoidable, by adopting as new
institutions those already obsolete elsewhere (privileged

companies, royal factories), or extending ancient ones (merchant guilds in Spain and the colonies), in attempting to renovate by multiplying concessions and privileges to a few instead of widening opportunity to those of talent, Iberian governments merely proliferated traditional structures of economy and society. They shored up the "gothic edifice," which was not precisely the way to ready it for great crises.

The collapse of adjustment by administrative fiat, the withering of zeal for guided change, the evaporation of a spirit of restrained innovation was accelerated by revolution in France. In the eighteenth century France had represented a Catholic monarchy capable of growth without the upheaval that Protestant England had endured during the seventeenth century. Anarchy in France signified to cautious Spanish gradualists that even guided change was dangerous. And while momentum for change continued into the 1790's there developed a revived interest in enduring Spanish tradition. So the defense of traditional Spanish structures in the face of regicide, anarchy, and mob-rule in France led Spain to sever its French alliance in 1793 and to join briefly with now politically conservative and anti-republican England to crush revolution in France. The English were not interested in renovating Spain, but in denying France its assistance; they preferred to weaken Spain to open the way to the penetration of the colonies in America. The English would tolerate no revitalized Spanish navy. It was the perception of English attitudes which led Spain to renew the alliance with France in 1796 and thereafter Spain squirmed between the millstones of Anglo-French conflict until it collapsed in 1808 before the invading French forces. By then the Portuguese royalty as wards of England had fled to security in the colony in Brazil.

It was inevitable that Spain and for that matter Portugal

abandon prudent adjustment after the French revolution. A policy of gradual concessions to colonial pressures and to English contrabanding there could not be reversed as readily. The mining colonies such as Mexico and Peru could survive in wartime when Spanish shipping was eliminated from Atlantic sea-lanes because precious metals do not deteriorate in storage. For the products of areas where plantation and ranches had expanded in the eighteenth century in response to west European demand, warehousing for post-war shipment was scarcely possible. Sugar, tobacco, cacao, hides deteriorated rapidly while slaves who produced most of them had to be fed with imports of United States salt fish, salt beef, flour—and replaced by English and United States slaving vessels. In areas such as Havana, Caracas, and Buenos Aires merchant guilds, unlike those of Mexico City, Veracruz, and Lima, were often split between agricultural and ranching interests and representatives of the alliance with Cadiz. It was difficult for Spanish colonial administrators to force upon these guilds a policy of commercial self-restraint when the English severed communication with Europe, all the more when many colonial entrepreneurs participated eagerly in illegal trading with the English. Gradual concessions to colonial economic pressures had in effect expanded the patterns of economic dependence in the American colonies vis-à-vis western Europe, and after 1800 vis-à-vis England. The Spaniards had reluctantly enouraged only a minimum of colonial interregional trade. In sum, the policy of compartmentalization of the colonies, of tardy recognition of the possibilities of export agriculture and ranching, of excessive preoccupation with silver mining, exacerbated the pressures in the colonies between 1802 and 1808, between Amiens and the French invasion.

Finally, one should never underestimate the sense of independence among the criollo elite after the successful rebellion against British rule in North America and the possibilities of criollo political control inherent in the ideology of the French revolution. Under Napoleon, France seemed to reconcile popular sovereignty, monarchy, slavery, and the slave trade. The Spanish colonial elite learned quickly of the flight of the Portuguese royal family to Brazil and the immediate opening of Brazil's ports to the ships of friendly and allied nations. Once the authority of monarchy collapsed in Spain with the abdication of the Spanish Bourbons, the colonial elite was impatient for effective political control within or without an imperial structure. A policy of tardy adjustment, the Spaniards and criollos in America now perceived, was an irreversible process. It could be dammed, even diverted for a time, but inevitably it pressed through all barriers. Or so it seemed between 1808 and 1810.

4

> But there is one all-important point which should claim our attention, and that is the conservation of our Americas . . . What Authority should they obey? Which Province should send out the orders necessary for their government, for the appointment and direction of their administrators, and other points indispensable to the maintenance of their dependence? . . . each Colony will establish its independent Government . . . its natural inclination to independence may well lead to it. . . . This consideration alone shows that the establishment of a Supreme Authority, and a National Representation is not only indispensable, but most urgent.
>
> Junta de Valencia, 16 July 1808

*The Junta [Central] declared that it considered the American
dominions integral and essential parts of the Spanish monarchy; and America neither perceived nor could perceive in
this declaration the source of rights it should always have
enjoyed and which could never have been denied without
injustice; rather [Americans] viewed it as a solemn confession
of the despotism by which they had until then been tyrannized.*

Junta de Caracas to the Regency,
3 May 1810

*The equality of rights conceded to the Americans does not
carry with it all those which peninsular Spaniards enjoy or
may enjoy . . . Is it not true that within European Spain itself some provinces have enjoyed freedoms and many exemp-
tions denied to others? . . . the equality which has been
established is not absolute. . . . Such a proposal . . . would
do away with what is left of the trade of European Spain.*

Consulado de Cadiz to the Cortes,
7 June 1811

The twenty-two months between November 1807 and September 1810 were perhaps the most decisive in the history of
Iberian America since the conquest. Contemporaries in Paris
and London, Lisbon and Madrid and in America in Mexico
City, Havana, Caracas, Rio de Janeiro, and Buenos Aires
recognized this fact immediately. No longer could a major
dynastic change with all its implications for contending
pressure groups occur in Spain without setting off colonial
repercussions. The population and resources of Iberian
America which, in reciprocal fashion, responded to and in
turn stimulated European economic growth in the eighteenth century, were now essential not only to the underdeveloped Portuguese and Spanish metropolitan economies
but also to the two major economic blocs competing for west
European hegemony, the blocs dominated by England and

France. In order to stiffen with silver inlays the backs of its European allies the English needed desperately direct access to Mexico's bullion; they needed hides and cotton for industrial production, and they wanted direct access to the hundreds of thousands of consumers in Iberian America. The French co-prosperity sphere imposed upon Europe as the continental system only heightened English impatience with the Spanish and Portuguese colonial policy of excluding foreigners from direct participation. French merchants, manufacturers, and financiers as well as policy-makers, now expected Napoleon to secure comparable access.

The effective English blockade of the peninsula and the advance of French troops toward Portugal and Andalusia threatened to cut irreparably the peninsula's lifeline to America. These pressures shattered the *modus vivendi* with France and made imperative alliance with England. However, doubts about the response of colonial elites to policy decisions in Lisbon and Madrid were a nightmare to metropolitan crisis-managers. Delicate enough was the balance in the metropolises between those willing and those unwilling to make concessions to American interests or in the colonies. What was worse, the colonial elites—wealthy, powerful, affected by the flow of information from France, England, and the United States—were increasingly ready to consider alternatives.

A century after Utrecht the focal points of Iberian America were no longer limited to areas of silver exports, Peru and Mexico. Now Lisbon and Madrid policy-makers had to consider the interests of exporters of colonial agricultural and ranching products. By November 1807, too, the Portuguese at Lisbon knew that acceptance of French occupation would trigger English intervention in Brazil. The English had given the Spaniards a foretaste of what their aggressive policy would be if Spain continued as an ally of France. In 1797 English troops had seized Trinidad; in 1806–07 they twice tried to occupy Buenos Aires; in late 1807 they spread rumors that an amphibious force was readying in Ireland for operations against Mexico.

It is the fate of colonial territories or states with dependent or externally oriented economies that while their internal pressures may often approach a breaking point, the decisive stimulus to change is generally external. The strain of repeated Anglo-French confrontation had in 1807 induced Napoleon to order the occupation of Portugal, the confiscation of English properties, and above all the seizure of the large number of Portuguese merchantmen in the capacious Lisbon harbor. The Portuguese royalty and court elite moved to the ships in the harbor and, escorted by English warships, fled to Rio de Janeiro. In January, the exiled Portuguese royalty broke the centuries-old Iberian colonial system by opening all Brazil's ports to direct access with friendly or neutral trading areas. In fact, this meant that England would now exploit the commerce of Brazil directly.

To Spanish colonial authorities news of the Portuguese exile and English economic preferment in Brazil was electrifying. English access to Brazil led inescapably to English economic infiltration in the La Plata basin, where contraband already flourished. Everywhere in Spanish America pressure was mounting to eliminate at last an irrational trading system based upon peninsular monopoly and contraband. What would be the impact of opening Brazil to direct trade? Of even greater importance to Spanish crisis managers and colonial interests was the removal of the seat of dynasty to America, for not only did such a move presage bypassing of the peninsular commercial entrepot; it meant the removal of all legislative, judicial, and executive, not least of all appointive, power to America. Such a contingency had long been seen as catastrophic for Spain.

Then, between March and May 1808 the Spanish Bourbons disappeared from the apex of government, and what Spanish bureaucrats had long dreaded materialized: the collapse of central authority, rebellion, and the refractioning of the Spains into competing regions, and the possibility that colonial areas in America would follow the path of the Spains toward local administration or juntas. Most frightening was the prospect that self-constituted juntas in the colonies would in the absence of any countervailing central administration be empowered to make economic decisions disastrous for the metropolitan economy.

For the criollo elites at the various colonial pressure points the moment of truth had come. As the recent history of colonialism suggests, the manifold material and psychological ties of dependence between colony and imperial power no matter how attenuated are not lightly cast off. The traditionalists in the colonies—Spanish merchants, bureaucrats, churchmen, military—banked upon what they often stressed as the ties of kinship, language, and religion linking European and American Spaniards to uphold the imperial system. In fact, they believed the fundamental tie was the right of conquest and the right to dispose of the colonies' resources. They were concerned that even the mildest form of commercial liberty would widen the yawning chasm of divergent economic interests. To many criollos the imperial system meant more than exploitation, on the other hand; it permitted them to share with the Spaniards in the colonies control over labor, wealth, income, prestige, and power. So most criollos preferred to await signs of a metropolitan readiness to make necessary adjustments in the colonial system, to gratify criollo pressure groups, and to tinker with parts while preserving the major structural elements of shared privilege and exploitation.

Decision to divorce colony from metropolis, slowed by such inhibitions, did not come immediately; rather it was reached slowly, the outcome of successive events in Spain and America. Gradually criollos perceived that desired changes in the colonies would be denied them by the new authorities in Spain. The first political group to claim leadership in unoccupied Spain, the Junta de Sevilla (May–September 1808), quickly revealed its grasp of colonial reality by unilaterally arrogating to itself control over the colonies and by maintaining intact the colonial trading system. To dissuade the criollos from direct action via the formation of local juntas or congresses, Sevilla sent to Havana, Mexico, and Caracas in the summer of 1808 agents directed to order the imprisonment of colonial leaders contemplating pacifying criollo elites with the formation of juntas. Someruelos, captain-general of Cuba, barely escaped deposition. Iturrigaray in Mexico was not as supple and was deposed by a group of conspirators recruited from the Spanish mercantile community in Mexico City; he was then sent off to prison at Cadiz under the charge of treason. At Caracas leading criollos advocating a junta were arrested in November 1808 and an honorary judge of the audiencia was shipped to Spain for trial. To many criollos this display of authority in the form of naked force was instructive and chastening.

Sevilla represented the Andalusian agricultural and mer-

cantile interest with an old stake in the preservation of the
colonial empire in America. Centuries of contact with the
colonies, of investment and participation in trade, mines,
and estates, of employment in government service and the
church, of dependence upon pensions paid by colonial trea-
suries—this was the stake now threatened. The Spanish traditionalists at home and in the colonies turned to the Junta
of Sevilla and its ties to Cadiz for maintenance of the status
quo. But more perceptive groups and less privileged areas of
the peninsula turned to the Junta Central which superseded
the Sevillan Junta in September 1808 and which represented
a national over a regional interest and, to the criollos, appeared readier to bow to the law of colonial necessity, specif-
ically, to modify the colonial trading system. By mid-1809,
after a period of vacillation, the colonists learned that the
Junta Central was considering a general policy of opening
colonial ports to limited direct contact with friendly and
neutral nations in Spanish ships.

The Junta Central's readiness to contemplate revision of
the system of trade, following its refusal to uphold the colonial prerogatives of the Junta de Sevilla, and the increasing
antagonism between it and the Junta de Cadiz over financial
and commercial affairs were important factors in its dissolu-
tion. The anxious criollos in America were shocked by its
final collapse and replacement by a Regency which, fleeing
to Cadiz, the last corner of unoccupied Spain, soon became a
captive if not a creature of the Junta de Cadiz dominated by
merchant guild members. In colonial America the patience
and expectations of criollos ended and revolutionary juntas
in the name of autonomy appeared at Caracas (April) and
Buenos Aires (May) and a mass insurrection began in the

Mexican hinterland near the chief mining center of Guanajuato in September.

This was only the first stage of a long, bloody struggle which lasted more than a decade, often with heavy overtones of civil war. Many Americans had perceived that an inequitable system could effectively be transformed only by recourse to violent overthrow of existing structures, and that defensive modernization did nothing but preserve the essence of a traditional society and economy that was now intolerable.

5

". . . The perverse and ambitious ideas of obscure and despicable men [in America] who, unable to elevate themselves from their mean status by virtues they lack, hoped to improve their condition at the expense of the luckless land they soiled with their crimes."

Merchants of Cadiz, "Memoria sobre las
operaciones de la Comisión de Reemplazos,"
1832

"No one dares to distinguish them [castas]. This would be odious information and in executing it with rigor we would discover in well-accepted families dark stains that time has rubbed out, with the necessary result that we would have scandalous cases without end in our courts. . . ."

Padrón de Texcoco, 1753

"The Creoles and Mestizoes form, by their union, their numbers and their property, the principal force, and most respectable part of the Spanish colonists. As they have the same

interests to maintain, and the same grievances to redress, it
is probable that, in the event of any civil dissensions, they
would act together, whether against Indians or Europeans."

Edinburgh Review, 1810

Revolution in America occurred in 1810 because the criollo elite finally provided the leadership that the castas and the lower even more oppressed strata of colonial society had long awaited. To those who have examined the process of economic development and social change in a historical context it is clear that social systems appear to have extraordinary powers of cohesion, flexibility, adaptation. The cohesion of Latin American colonial social structures was maintained, if transformed, during three centuries largely because no viable alternative system appeared. Fidelity to Spain, sanctified by religious injunction, cemented the structure of colonial society, economy, and polity. The principle of hierarchy, of superordinate and subordinate social groups tied to the European metropolises, was accepted since it satisfied the interests and aspirations of an elite which, in effect, had the monopoly of force to maintain it.

In deciding to break with metropolitan controls, the colonial elite found natural allies in the mestizos, mulattoes, and castas in general; the Indian masses they handled gingerly. The Indians recognized their exploitation under the colonial system, but their bitterness had never successfully found effective expression. The criollo leaders now feared the masses, who often erupted in urban and rural violence, and they rationalized their repression and exploitation of them with the myth that they were inferiors. Undoubtedly some of the colonial elite believed that the Indian masses might remain inert in case of rebellion or, if mobilized intelligently, could be controlled to aid in the elimination of the handful of Spanish bureaucrats and merchants. Support by the castas strengthened the elite's position and promised assistance in controlling the Indians. With the backing of the castas, who were perhaps even more irked by the Spanish-imposed social hierarchy and by restrictions on "passing" and upon economic activity, some of the colonial elite probably saw the possibility of a rather peaceful transition toward independence. In allying with the castas, they co-opted a small but influential social group whose role was magnified by the expansion and diversification of the eighteenth-century colonial economy and by demographic growth.

Put another way, one detects in eighteenth-century Latin America the transformation of the older bases of colonial hierarchy, estates and corporations, into something approximating economic classes based upon wealth and income. The castas seem to have grown proportionately faster than the other social groups, and the lighter-skinned castas moved upward into the group of what were now called American Spaniards. In a word, "passing" became easier and more widespread. Castas were accepted in the colonial militia where criollo officers predominated. The large and growing intermediate group of mestizos and mulattoes spilled over from the hacienda and the Indian communities to fill the expanding number of occupations a diversifying economy requires. They resented the social stigma a colonial regime fastened upon them because of their "inferior" social origins. They bribed local priests to register their children as Spaniards rather than as light mulattoes or light mestizos, or they later had parish records changed. European officials at the end of the eighteenth century complained of the difficulty of registering people as castas for tax purposes. Nor could castas be kept out of artisan guilds nor even kept from pursuing artisan production outside them. They became weavers who established their own weaving shops; they became shopkeepers and itinerant merchants; they entered the church in large numbers; they flowed into the lesser bureaucracy. In colonial areas of heavy slave importation in the eighteenth century the number of free Negroes and mulattoes increased proportionately. It is not that racial prejudice declined: it is simply that rigid maintenance of status based upon color and ancestry became too difficult. To some extent the sheer number and diversity of castas tended to create a new basis of hierarchy, wealth, at the end of the colonial period. Those able to break away from the status of slave, those who abandoned the Indian communities or indigenous enclaves of Amerinds, became a middle group which could survive only by ruthless pursuit of self-interest. The Hispanized Indian or ladino, the mestizo, the free Negro, became in many cases a more ruthless exploiter of his social inferiors than the White elite. This was becoming evident before the wars of independence; it was to become even clearer afterward.

If the major legacy of colonial society was degradation and social conflict, what basis exists then for the often heard view that the Iberians had a policy toward Indians and Negroes which was more humanitarian and more tolerant than that of the non-Catholic west Europeans in America? It is true that there were sensitive, articulate, and hardheaded churchmen in the colonies who perceived the deculturizing, brutalizing, and exploitative aspects of culture-contact and imperialism in the sixteenth century. Such a man was Las Casas. One must, however, recall that other clerics who left posterity detailed ethnographic accounts of the social, political, and religious history of the conquered peoples of America studied the major institutions and values of dominated peoples in order to make colonial rule enduring. They were applied anthropologists. This, after all, was the aim of Las Casas' clerical contemporaries, Landa and Saha-gun. If they often admired the institutions described, the admiration was given grudgingly.

Iberian colonialism did not exterminate subject peoples. It did accept the people of miscegenation. It did tolerate a degree of slave manumission. Yet the direction of colonial rule was not toward social uplift, toward integration; colo-nial rule was predicated upon separation, not integration, whether one examines tax systems, access to political or mili-tary office, even the church. Limited social integration and racial toleration were by-products of special conditions, in particular, the shortage of free labor available for interstitial occupations, those between field hand and elite. Since few Europeans were available to fill these jobs, the colonial soci-ety had to supply them. Hence the number of mestizos and mulattoes accepted at certain levels of society, in certain occupational roles. The fact that access to high status and occupation was rigidly controlled permitted the absorption of some newcomers.

The pre-eminent social legacy of colonialism was the deg-radation of the labor force, Indian and Negro, everywhere in Latin America. This is the abiding significance of debt peonage and chattel slavery. That occasionally members of the mixed groups were incorporated into the ruling group during the colonial period or distinguished themselves in the struggle for independence is not a persuasive argument for the racial integration of either colonial or post-colonial soci-ety. To argue in this fashion is to raise random sexual activ-ity to the level of planned parenthood and to consider the growth of a mestizo or mulatto population a reliable index of racial integration and equality. On the contrary, it might be argued that the rigor of the barriers to upward social mobility—the barriers of birth, color, and economic deprivation in both colonial and post-colonial Latin America—permitted the elite to absorb an insignificant percentage of the more aggressive mixed groups and thereby to preserve the essence of social stratification. Absorption into the elite meant that newcomers accepted the social values and aspirations of that group; in striving for higher status, they lost contact with the disadvantaged groups which they abandoned and simultaneously removed themselves as leaders of the struggle for the amelioration of the lot of the illiterate, impoverished masses of color.

To be sure, social aspects of colonialism cannot be divorced from the economic matrix, and the heart of that matrix in Latin America remained privilege in the form of access to property and occupation, to ownership of mines, large farms, cattle ranches, to trade, and to the bureaucracy. A stratified and hierarchical society meant that a small group closely interrelated by marriage and kinship controlled wealth and income. Failure to diversify the colonial economy meant that economic opportunity remained limited. For the masses there was no role other than that of field hands or urban proletariat. And those who labored as dependents, debt peons or chattel slaves, were stigmatized as inferior. Rationalization buttressed inferiority. Indians were ignorant, superstitious, docile, lacking intelligence and initiative, not because society made them so, but because they were Indians—so thought the elite. Similarly they rationalized the maintenance of Negro slavery on the grounds that Christianity saved the Negro from barbarism and tribal warfare. To educate such elements of congenital backwardness was an exercise in futility. The colonial legacy of social degradation and racial prejudice surfaced in the nineteenth century in the form of acute racial pessimism, in the belief that only the immigration of European Whites via colonization could supply the industrious labor force capable of effectively transforming Latin America.

Social realities have a habit, however, of proving rationalizations of the *status quo* inadequate. We are now beginning to realize that much of the social unrest of Latin America in the past century was a continuation of conflicts over access to property and occupation that the lower classes touched off in the eighteenth century, that flared up briefly in the struggles for independence and which the elite suppressed after 1824. It is in the twentieth century that the long struggle for social vindication, rooted in the colonial past, is again re-emerging.

PART THREE

The Nineteenth Century

CHAPTER V

The Economic Basis of Neo-colonialism

1

"The vast kingdom of New Spain, if cultivated with care, would alone produce what the rest of the world produces, sugar, cochineal, cacao, cotton, coffee, wheat, hemp, linen, silk, oil, wine. It would supply all the metals, without excluding mercury.

A. von Humboldt, *Essai politique*, 1807

In the early decades of the nineteenth century Europeans' reports of the untapped natural resources of Latin America nourished the view that technology and capital from abroad would stimulate the development of Latin America and thus help it to cast off the institutions, attitudes, and values which constituted the colonial heritage. Alexander von Humboldt's four-volume work on Mexico began to appear at Paris in 1807, before the outbreak of revolutionary movements. It was the first work of a notable nineteenth-century genre which, by highlighting the chasm between resource potential and inadequate level of economic exploitation, suggested that Latin America would not long continue its economic dependence, underdevelopment, or backwardness with respect to the North Atlantic area. We know now that with rare exceptions ex-colonial nations do not readily escape from the heritage of dependence.

While nations, like individuals, cannot escape their heritage, it is within their power to modify it substantially or moderately. In the case of post-colonial Latin America, the colonial heritage was subjected, as it is today, to pressures for change. We will approach post-colonial developments from two perspectives: first, the economic structures and their modification or elaboration, and second, political structures, the role of ideology, and social change.

A caveat is in order. It will be difficult to generalize as facilely for the post-colonial period of the nineteenth century as we have for the colonial period. Generalizations are usually misleading, particularly when they deal with so vast an area in which over-all control has disappeared, where topography is varied and sometimes nearly insurmountable, where resource endowments are unequal, where the ethnic composition of the population is so variegated, and where the constellations of interest or pressure groups have been so dissimilar, and these differences do not take into account divergent pre-conquest legacies and colonial development patterns. If generalizations are sometimes useful, substantive material is more so. To provide substance, then, examples will be drawn from widely divergent areas, primarily Mexico, Brazil, and Argentina.

2

"... The United States cannot exchange with Europe on equal terms; and the want of reciprocity would render them the victim of a system which would induce them to confine their views to Agriculture, and refrain from Manufactures. A constant and increasing necessity, on their part, for the com-

*modities of Europe, and only a partial and occasional demand
for their own, in return, could not but expose them to a state
of impoverishment. . . ."*

A. Hamilton, *Report on Manufactures*, 1791

*A newer garden of creation, no primal solitude,
Dense, joyous, modern, populous millions, cities and farms,
With iron interlaced, composite, tied, many in one,
By all the world contributed—freedom's and law's and thrift's
    society,
The crown and teeming paradise, so far, of time's accumula-
    tions,
To justify the past.*

W. Whitman, "The Prairie States,"
Leaves of Grass, 1855

For an analysis of the historical dimension of economic
change in Latin America, one might raise a question at the
outset: Why did two once-colonial areas, the United States
and Latin America, develop such markedly contrasting patterns of economic growth after independence? Why did the
United States by 1870 emerge as perhaps the second industrial nation of the world in value of manufacturing output,
while Latin America still remained primarily a major producer of colonial staples, raw materials, and foodstuffs for
the North Atlantic basin? Comparative economic history is
still in its infancy, even among English and French historians, and it remains more suggestive than definitive.
At best it is a clumsy tool in Latin American history, where
basic studies in agricultural, commercial, and banking history are lacking, and where political treatments, on the
whole, do not deal with national, sectional, and international pressure groups. Yet even the crudest of comparisons
may raise significant questions.

In seeking a basis for comparing the development of two major colonial areas after independence, one is led inevitably back to the European culture complexes from which English and Iberian colonists migrated and within which their models of society were conceived. It is not enough to compare the measure of local participation in colonial political processes, the degree of colonial censorship and toleration, the colonial view of education, the extent of colonial economic liberty; one must trace these elements to their European matrices. In contrast to Spain, as has been suggested earlier, English settlers in North America came from a modernizing England which generally treated literacy, toleration, individual rights, economic liberty, saving and investment as inseparable elements of the process of change and growth. Interaction of English and North American interest during the eighteenth century caused some of these elements to develop what many Europeans then considered an exaggerated virulence in parts of the colonies. There, in the absence of many inhibiting factors present in Europe and in other colonial areas, colonists were forced to seek new solutions to new problems and to adopt new and different patterns of thought and action.

Furthermore, the environment in which the English settled contrasted in essential ways with that of the first Iberian colonists. Though early English company charters provided for the discovery of mines of precious metals, no mines were found. And if they had, it might be asked, who would provide the labor to exploit them? This suggests a second factor determining the future development of the two areas: for west Europeans in North America did not have to confront or incorporate substantial Indian cultures; they pushed aside the nomadic Amerindian inhabitants, killed them, or isolated the survivors on unproductive lands as indigent wards of White society. The Indian of the United States remained unincorporated and unintegrated; for White society and economy his condition was and still is irrelevant and peripheral. For heuristic purposes, however, one might surmise that had Englishmen found a dense and highly organized Amerindian population, the history of what is called the United States would record the development of a stratified, bi-racial, very different society. In a larger context, the existence of a huge, underpopulated virgin land of extraordinary resource endowment directly facing Europe and enjoying a climate comparable to that of Europe represented a potentiality for development which existed nowhere else in the New World. The throw-offs of the revolutions of two centuries in Europe, land-hungry White emigrants of generally homogeneous culture, were peculiarly prepared to discard European tutelage and pursue the cumulative advantages of this conjuncture. Acquiring legal title to this vast real estate not always *before* occupation nor always in strictly legal ways, North Americans were ready to develop a variety of innovative techniques in its occupation and development.

External factors also played a major role in determining early political and economic growth in the United States. Long confined to the limited agricultural possibilities of the seaboard, the northern English colonies developed shipbuilding and mercantile activities, the latter particularly in the Caribbean after 1763, while the southern colonies created an export-oriented agriculture based upon slave labor. During the American Revolution two of Europe's foremost colonial powers provided what has been called decisive support to the English colonies in their bid to free themselves from their metropolis. It is as ironic that Mexico's silver and Saint Domingue's sugar helped emancipate the English colonies as it is that France's financial sacrifice for the American Revolution contributed to the French Revolution, and Spain's sacrifice created an example and model for the rebellion in its own colonies. In that war of liberation, the United States gave little to the insurgents and gained much from Spanish weakness: Florida, Alabama, and access to a vast trading area in Spanish America. Of great significance for the development of the United States after 1783 was the growth of trade with the ex-metropolis. First trade, then English investment helped develop the ex-colony's economy. By contrast, the liberated Spanish colonies found neither trade, nor financial, nor technical assistance in their underdeveloped, erstwhile metropolis.

A further external factor of significance in the consolidation and growth of the economy of the United States in the early years of its national existence was the opportunity presented by international conflict during the French Revolution and the era of Napoleon. By 1793 national policy had created the basis of banking and a capital market, while European conflict in the following twenty years provided opportunities for northeastern merchants, shipbuilders and shippers to enter the Atlantic carrying trade as neutrals handling traffic between the United States and Europe, exporting southern cotton and rice, and re-exporting Caribbean sugar, coffee, cacao. Returns from these operations reinforced the financial infrastructure, and during the slump in the carrying trade, 1808 to 1814, idle resources were applied to textile manufacture. After 1814 external demand for cotton and in the 1830's rising export prices stimulated the South's concentration upon cotton production for export, which constituted 50 per cent by value of United States exports to western Europe and the northeastern United States until the Civil War.

The North became a financial center for southern agriculture, an entrepôt for its imports of manufactures and luxuries, and a supplier of manufactures such as cotton textiles and iron goods. After 1830 the occupation and settlement of western lands increased the Northeast's importance as exporter of western grains, and widened the markets for the Northeast's industrial output. But the westward expansion of slavery also threatened the North and led to one of the bloodiest civil wars of modern times. By the outbreak of the Civil War, economic growth in the United States had been sparked by external factors and by the creation of a national market despite the chattel slavery of the South. More relevant to the comparison with Latin America, the Civil War further opened the way to the industrialization of the United States.

3

"Somber events engulf us; although the revolution is over, its consequences keep us exposed to grave perils; various parties, some swollen by triumph, others bitter over defeat, divide our reborn society; the methods and channels of public wealth are weak. . . ."

El Aguila Mexicana, 1823

"One cannot exaggerate the state of misery to which the Republic has been reduced [after years of warfare in Uruguay]. Between Minas and Maldonado the traveler encounters only sky and grass. Not even 500 cattle or horses did I see in that

strip of land 16 leagues long. There are estancieros who sub-
sist on jerked beef and rice, and one who can offer you roast
meat cannot be called poor."

Pedro Bustamante, 1853

By contrast, the colonial heritage and external conditions
before, during, and after independence in Latin America
both created new and exacerbated old conflicts of interest
which remained unresolved for decades after 1824 and led to
the option of internal war rather than constitutional compromise. When French armies invaded the Iberian peninsula, the English chose to make the peninsula a bleeding
ground of French continental military supremacy; long
smoldering colonial conflicts erupted in a series of discon-
nected, continent-wide civil wars between 1810 and 1824.
Early, two major currents in all anti-colonial wars fused: resistance to further transatlantic economic control and struggle over who would then rule at home. The Spanish colonial
policy of ruling by dividing, of balancing one interest group
against the other, collapsed in 1810. It left a colonial legacy
of sectional and regional conflict.

It is widely held that the Latin American independence
movements were aimed at ending metropolitan monopoly of
economic decision-making and that therefore they represent
a struggle for economic liberty. No one can deny that this is
what they achieved, but it would be a gross oversimplification to state that this was the principal goal of the early insurgents. In fact, acceptance of this generalization has
clouded the interpretation of the post-independence decades.
Perhaps it would be more accurate to argue that many of the
colonial elite hoped to maintain allegiance to embattled
Spain while enjoying the right to trade directly with all Europe and the United States. They did not desire to overturn

society but rather to enlarge somewhat access to, and enjoyment of, positions of profitable monopoly. Open conflict ensued when Spanish intractability on the key issue of direct trade was backed by Spanish readiness to employ military force against the reformers.

Segments of the elite in colonial Latin America were attempting in effect to make the colonial economic system rational for their interests. While the United States by 1793 could profit from European conflict, the Spanish colonies were both stimulated and frustrated. Their output of sugar, cacao, coffee, hides, and salt beef rose, but Spanish shipping was interrupted by the omnipresent British navy, and Spanish colonial policy had blocked the creation of a shipping industry in the colonies. Foodstuffs and manufactures were denied the colonies, and could be obtained only by massive participation in smuggling with English and United States ships off their coasts. Hence the mounting pressure for direct trade, for legalizing reality. But when independence solved the problem of direct trade, there was no political nor economic unity to permit rapid utilization of economic decision-making. Serious internal disunity, in fact, prolonged the civil wars of independence.

Hence post-independence decades were wasted in trying to settle highly divisive problems imbedded in the colonial heritage. The most conspicuous of the Spanish and Portuguese colonial elite, military officers, high bureaucrats, merchants—the core of opposition to independence—emigrated. A large majority remained, a significant contrast with the high percentage of émigrés from the new United States and from revolutionary France. In the immediate post-independence decades the influence of well-connected enclaves of such traditionalists upon Latin America was decisive. The new national capitals, generally the hub of the colonial economic network, wished to maintain their monopolistic position in national and international trade. To them, this was the reward of independence. But the sub-regions, many of which had developed in the eighteenth century, often stimulated by contraband activities, insisted on regional economic autonomy; this is why they often became federalists, not centralists. In Mexico, Guadalajara attacked the Mexico City–Veracruz commercial axis; in Argentina, the western interior provinces resisted expansionist Buenos Aires, and they were joined by the Litoral provinces and by Uruguay and Paraguay, former divisions of the colonial viceroyalty. The western provinces of Argentina wished to protect the local production of cotton, woolen, and linen textiles, leather goods, sugar, wines, and brandies. Having lost access to former markets in what was now Bolivia, they sought to expand in the new Argentina. But Buenos Aires merchants were interested solely in selling cheaper European imports. The conflict of regional economic interests versus those of the older mercantile centers was repeated everywhere in Latin America.

In Mexico those involved in the artisan textile industry wanted to preserve the national market for their output, but the Mexico City merchants preferred to import English manufactured products. In sum, the new nations were torn by conflicts: between those who wished to monopolize all domestic and foreign trade from one national point and those who sought a local distribution monopoly; between those who wished to protect local artisan production, and those who distributed cheaper imports; between those who favored agriculture and those who favored mining or industry. Each sub-area under the assumed protection of federal

constitutions and provincial or state autonomy sought to
create regional economic enclaves by internal tariffs or tolls.
Thus no national unity was readily forged; there was no immediate possibility of a unified, national economic policy as
was created early in the United States.

In any event, other factors would have made it difficult to
escape the combined legacy of colonialism and civil war.
After independence attempts to create new industries were
hampered by the absence of banking institutions and capital
markets and by the low level of capital accumulation. Civil
war had destroyed livestock and estates, dispersed manpower, disrupted the mines. The major sources of funds, the
church and the merchants, were reluctant to diversify investment. Industries' in underdeveloped areas do not make demand, they respond to it. And the nature of the colonial economy of Latin America, like that of the southern United
States, had concentrated income, held the per capita income
of the masses at a minimal level and inhibited capital formation in liquid assets; in a word, it reduced the possibility of
sustained local demand for high cost products of infant
industry. Massive imports of British manufactures simply
crushed local industry based upon primitive technology.
Inevitably, like the southern United States, Latin America
was drawn to the search for export staples, traditional or
new, to pay for imports. It was drawn to the land and to
external sources of dynamism.

In this way, the colonial economic heritage was reinforced
by local conditions and, in particular, by the economic pressure of Great Britain, which now harvested more than a
century of sustained interest in the Iberian colonial world.
British manufacturers, merchants, bankers, insurance companies, shippers—all consolidated their success in the struggle

against French competitors. Everywhere in Latin America, British merchants entrenched themselves—in Buenos Aires, Rio de Janeiro, Valparaiso, Caracas, in Veracruz, Cartagena, Lima. Great Britain, technologically and industrially advanced, became as important to the Latin American economy as to the cotton-exporting southern United States. At this point, Latin America fell back upon traditional export activities, utilizing the cheapest available factor of production, the land, and the dependent labor force. The land in Mexico, Brazil, and Argentina emerged as what it had always been, a source of security, income, prestige, and power.

The achievement of economic self-determination in ex-colonial areas does not necessarily lead to its efficient long-term use. The failure of Latin American movements for independence to create the bases of sustained economic growth through balanced agricultural, ranching, and industrial diversification only indicates the continued strength of a colonial heritage of externally oriented economies linked closely to essential sources of demand and supply outside the new national economies. This colonial heritage has a parallel in the southern United States after independence that is heartening even in a negative fashion. It suggests that an export-oriented economy based upon the large-scale production of staples by a coerced labor force has resilience, even when it exists in the same nation-state with its antithesis, a modern, egalitarian, industrializing economy and society. The South was an internal colony of the mercantile, industrial, and financial North. Yet even in the South paternalism, elitism, and plantation agriculture have ensured until recent times the survival of institutions and attitudes, ways of living and thinking, which come remarkably close to those of other plantation areas of the New World. The colonial heritage has effectively delayed the formation of what we term today modernized societies.

Ex-colonies, then and now, cannot readily shed the economic legacy of centuries of colonialism, they cannot rapidly close the gap between backwardness and modernity, between primitive and advanced technology, between low and high levels of income, saving, and investment, between literacy and illiteracy, between obscurantism and enlightenment, between closed and open societies, between—as the sociologists phrase it—societies based upon adscription and those based upon achievement. It is not surprising, then, that Latin America did not begin to modernize its economy through industrialization until a century after independence.

Under these circumstances the major consequence of the anti-colonial movements in Latin America between 1810 and 1824, the crushing of the ties of transatlantic empire, led— one is almost tempted to say, inevitably—to neo-colonialism. Leaving aside for the moment socio-political and psychological elements of the colonial heritage, we can see how the economic growth of Latin America through diversification and industrialization could not occur while colonial patterns of production, capital accumulation and investment, income distribution and expenditure survived. We are now readier to accept the fact that institutional factors or barriers play a determining—perhaps *the* determining—role in affecting the rate of economic and social change. Thus, in all the major areas of Latin America after 1824 there emerged a search for a viable basis of export economies, for the production and export of primary products or, as they were then termed, "colonial staples." Not until about a half-century after independence was the new basis firmly established, and its establishment coincided with the onset of political stability. Yet political stability in whatever form it takes—republic or monarchy—may be a necessary, but not a sufficient basis for economic sovereignty. The absence of an autonomous, self-sustaining economy strengthened the heritage or heritages of colonialism in Latin America after 1824. This is the rationale that Latin Americans and others have evoked in calling post-colonial Latin American economy and society neo-colonial.

4

The most significant heritage of Iberian colonialism was the tradition of the large estate, producing foodstuffs and raw materials for local consumption or for export to western Europe. In the case of colonial Mexico, hacienda production of beef, hides, corn, wheat, pulque, or sugar and its derivatives was directed almost exclusively toward a large internal market. In Brazil the sugar engenho with its cane fields, grinding mills, and boilers had dominated the agricultural sector from the end of the sixteenth century, and sugar exports from the northeast, primarily the Bahia-Pernambuco area, were still important around 1800. In Argentina at the same time large estancias or cattle ranches exporting hides and tallow dominated the pampa, or prairie, around the port of Buenos Aires. The large estate characterized by family ownership and management, the residence of the extended family, the living and working area for often hundreds of dependents, was more than a unit of production. It represented a type of social organization, a source of social prestige and political power, as well as wealth and income. Only in east-

ern Europe could there be found estates analogous to those
found in Latin America and the southern United States. The
large landed estate symbolized security; above all, it held the
promise of continuity through the preservation of status
from generation to generation.

Until the twentieth century the basis of oligarchy in Latin
America has been the monopolization of, and access to, land
ownership. In fact, the most significant feature of the history
of land tenure there until very recent decades has been the
spread of the large estate into frontier areas, or the ag-
grandizement of long established estates, if not for control
over cultivable lands or scarce water rights, then for control
of scarce labor, agricultural manpower. In Latin America,
the nineteenth century may be viewed as a period of acceleration in the rate of estate formation and estate owners'
control over manpower. For different reasons, this process
occurred in Cuba, Argentina and, in a particularly acute
form, in Mexico and Brazil.

5

*"One of [Mexican agriculture's] greatest drawbacks is that
the whole country is divided up into immense haciendas or
landed estates, small farms being rarely known; and, out of
a population of ten millions or more, the title to the soil (apart
from the lands held by the Indian communities) is said to vest
in not more than 5 or 6 thousand persons. Some of these
estates comprise square leagues instead of square acres in extent and are said to have irrigating ditches from 40 to 50
miles in length."*

D. A. Wells, *A Study of Mexico*, 1887

"The formula has been everywhere [in Mexico] almost the same, especially in recent times. They tell the Indian who owns land they will dispossess him and send him into the army because he has failed to pay his tax. The Indian does not know he does not have to pay and he hurries off to the local lawyer. The lawyer, in league with the local cacique, feeds upon his client's dread. . . . Finally, he offers him 4 reales for his property. . . . Of course, the Indian accepts and his small patrimony swells the pocket of the cacique; . . . this is the pattern of inequities that passes under the sublime name of Peace."

El País, 1908

To many observers at the end of the eighteenth century, concentration of land ownership in Mexico presaged potential conflict between landlords and the dependent resident labor force, or the nearby Indian communal enclaves. During the fiercely fought anti-colonial struggle in the years 1810 to 1821, agricultural and livestock estates were ravaged but were never parceled out by either side, and the decision of the Mexican elite to terminate Spain's transatlantic controls eliminated any possibility of land reform. It has been claimed that the end of legal social stratification, in which Indians occupied a ward-like status, gave them citizenship but stripped them of protection against capitalistic pressures. While Indian status declined in the nineteenth century as Indian communities lost control over communal properties, this process had long been developing. There is no doubt, however, that the republican legislation of Mexico in the nineteenth century transformed religious properties, public lands, and Indian communal holdings into large privately owned estates on an unprecedented scale, some argue on a scale unequaled in the history of any other country in modern times. By 1910 a number of interrelated factors had turned Mexico into a nation in which 3 per cent of the surveyed properties, that is, about 13,000 properties, controlled 58 per cent of the nation's surface.

First, of course, was the colonial tradition of the large estate which continued unchanged under the republic. Next was the failure to develop successful alternative enterprises as a field for investment and entrepreneurial skill. Mining operations never regained the level of prosperity enjoyed in 1810 until after 1880 when railroad transport, foreign capital, and imported technology were applied to silver mines and especially to other nonferrous minerals in northern Mexico. In the 1830's the government did establish through a national development bank a series of cotton textile spinning and weaving mills to absorb thousands of artisan textile workers faced with chronic unemployment as a result of large textile imports. The success was only moderate and there were few linkage effects to stimulate basic industry or to provide employment for about 23,000 workers. Apparently the level of mass income could not absorb the high unit costs of an industry sheltered by a prohibitive tariff structure.

In the third place, despite the stratified social structure inherited from the colony, post-independence Mexico contained a small, urban, articulate middle class that formed a Liberal core of opposition to colonial legacies. To the professionals, bureaucrats, and intellectuals of this group, guilds and monopolies stifled the birth of a new society. They viewed the church as a guild employing landed properties and income to resist rather than assist social and economic change. The church supported political regimes that stressed preservation of the *status quo,* protected the rights of such corporate holdovers as military and ecclesiastical courts of justice, maintained ecclesiastical control over public education, and favored immigration policy designed to exclude non-Catholics. Perhaps 50 per cent of landed properties remained under ecclesiastical control.

Finally, the Liberal middle class tended to view the Indian communities as overly protected enclaves whose members utilized agricultural and ranching properties inefficiently. The middle class believed that ecclesiastical and communal properties were bulwarks of traditionalism. How could an effective middle class society of small, independent, profit-oriented farmers be forged when large blocs of land were held by those unwilling or, perhaps worse, incapable of its efficient utilization? Here were all the ingredients of a sort of irrepressible conflict, and it flared up with the Liberal administration that swept Conservatives from control of the national government in 1854–55.

In 1856 and again in 1857 the Liberals legislated out of existence the real properties of civil and religious corporations not employed directly for the purposes of the corporation. Those renting or leasing such property from the church were to have first claim on its purchase, the price calculated by accepting annual rent as 6 per cent of real value. Unleased or unrented properties were to be sold at auction. The first careful analysis of the effect of the 1856 legislation corroborates generalizations long held about it. It reveals that of the 18 million pesos of transferred property values, 11.1 million or 61 per cent was communal property, that for the whole republic 1 per cent of those receiving properties occupied 33 per cent of all transferred properties by value, that roughly 50 persons now held new properties valued at 3.3 million pesos. Much of the property so transferred consisted of large estates; in the so-called grain basket state of Guanajuato the average sale value per property works out to

100,000 pesos. And most of the fifty new property owners were Mexicans, merchants or professionals. In retrospect the law of 1856 did not destroy land monopoly. At the expense of the church it provided new urban elements with access to the security and status of landed wealth. When Conservatives rejected the constitution of 1857 and precipitated civil war, church properties were nationalized and subsequently sold.

The impact of this legislation shattered Amerindian communal properties, many dating back to the pre-conquest period. The communities were forced by law to grant ownership to Amerinds tilling such holdings. In densely populated Central Mexico, despite attempts to slow application of the laws or to circumvent them, Amerindian properties began to disappear into the hands of politically powerful speculators, or they were absorbed by the neighboring larger estates, the haciendas. The rate of property transferral accelerated thirty years later. Between 1883 and 1894 as railroad construction spread a transport network over Mexico, inflating land values and attracting speculators, the national government resolved to accelerate the utilization of land by granting land surveying companies, many of them non-Mexican corporations, the right to survey all public lands as well as those without clear title for the purpose of subdivision and settlement, that is, for colonization by immigrants. One-third of the surveyed property was to accrue to the surveying corporations, who were empowered to purchase the remainder at special rates. Small property owners and surviving Indian pueblos, "those who could not call *compadre* a district judge, or a governor or a minister of state," were victimized in this process. In heavily populated Indian Oaxaca, for example, four concessionaires obtained more than 5.7 million acres. One analyst calculates that 134.5 million acres, or 27 per cent of the total area of the republic of Mexico were transferred to a few individuals.

These figures suggest the extent to which land monopoly advanced in nineteenth-century Mexico, and this impression is reinforced when it is realized that by the census of 1910 nearly 50 per cent of the total rural population, or 5.5 million debt peons, lived on approximately 8200 haciendas and 45,000 ranchos while about 50 per cent of the rural population was landless. In this fashion, neo-colonial Mexico completed the conquest of the land and the mobilization of the indigenous labor force for private profit with the assistance of the complex mechanisms of the modernizing state. There is more than a vague similarity between the widespread seventeenth-century Spanish confirmation of illegal and untitled landgrabbing and the role of the surveying companies and individual speculators at the end of the nineteenth century in Mexico.

It would be misapplied humanitarianism to claim that the Mexican elite under the regime of Porfirio Díaz—what Mexican scholars now term the *Porfiriato*—aimed to coerce the lower orders of society into semi-servile degradation. Land and labor policy under the Porfiriato represented an attempt, albeit a drastic one, to catch up with the modernizing and industrializing Western world, in particular with the aggressive, expansionist "cousin" to the north. Economic historians and developmental economists emphasize that industrialization cannot occur without comparable modernization of the agricultural sector so as to increase output to feed a growing population, to provide export earnings to finance import-substitution as well as an efficient infrastructure of transport, communications, bureaucracy, and social services.

It is from this perspective that massive land distribution in Mexico must be viewed, as a sort of classic, free-enterprise effort to modernize agriculture to further industrialization. Thus, it is part of a more complex process, one whereby the Mexican state maximized its assistance to private initiative by liberalizing access to mineral deposits, subsidizing the rapid formation of a railroad network linking mining sectors to points of export, and simultaneously creating for the first time a national market for domestic agricultural and industrial output. Estate owners were favored by protective tariffs against imports of cheaper foodstuffs while rural wage levels were frozen and labor supply augmented. Such economic policy and its application were the end product of nineteenth-century economic Liberalism, and at the apogee of the Porfirian economic boom Liberals openly admitted that the time had come for a temporary "honest tyranny."

Economic growth under these auspices, which its proponents term gradual and rational utilization of the factors of production and its opponents, the "cold rape of the pueblos and the heartless suppression of the small landowners," usually creates tensions that become intolerable to those bearing the burden of such modernization. In 1910 Mexico's experiment with this type of gradual economic growth turned into bloody civil war and ended in an unplanned social revolution which ultimately destroyed the colonial legacy of the hacienda. Until late in the twentieth century Mexico alone among Latin American nations had destroyed the symbols and reality of this ancient social and economic patrimony.

6

*"Of the three agents or factors of production—land, capital,
labor— . . . the Argentine Confederation has only land. . . .
Land is at this moment the supreme instrument at hand to
undertake the work of its population, political organization,
wealth and civilization."*

J. B. Alberdi, *Sistema económico
y rentístico de la Confederación
Argentina*, 1855

*"The Argentine Republic is presently a sort of gigantic estan-
cia that provides meat, wheat, butter, cotton and fruits that
Great Britain needs."*

Reconquista, 1939

Elsewhere in nineteenth-century Latin America large-scale
shifts of land from the public domain into private property
took place without the social effects visible in Mexico. Argentina emerged from colonial status with a vast hinterland
of prairie eminently suited to ranching and occupied by
nomadic Indians. Decades of bitter sectionalism delayed the
rapid growth of ranching exports until after 1853, when the
provinces achieved a federal republic. The economic content
of the constitution of 1853 was clear: development was the
goal; its means of achievement were the land, railroads, internal customs union, and immigrants now attracted by religious toleration.

By 1853 the colonial heritage of large cattle estancias had
been repeatedly reinforced by the renting and later sale of
public lands and by outright grant. In 1828 some 538 renters

received an average of 36,600 acres per holding, and between
1857 and 1862 another 233 renters each received 22,367 acres.
This only suggests the type of land distribution. Under a
colonization law, between 1868 and 1876 some 88 claimants
to public lands which were never colonized obtained over 5
million acres or 147,325 acres per claimant. In 1840 in the
pivotal province of Buenos Aires 825 estates controlled over
33 million acres, and by 1880 probably the best lands of all
Argentina were in large private holdings. There is perhaps a
more graphic way to illustrate the local effects of external
demand for Argentine hides and beef and wool. In 1836 a
square league of land in the province of Buenos Aires was
worth about 5,000 pesos while forty-three years later it had
risen to 200,000, and no improvements had been made in the
interim. By 1880, when 100,000 immigrants entered the
country, Argentina was a land of huge estates, the property
of a landholding oligarchy which needed and yet despised
immigrants. The carbine settled the problem of nomadic Indians on the pampas as efficiently as on the western prairies
of the United States. In about fifty years a combination of
colonial land tenure patterns, external demand, and the international division of labor incorporated Argentina into the
world economy and transformed her into one of the wealth-
iest, most integrated and "modernizing" economies of Latin
America.

7

"Wherever slavery is examined, it will be seen that it swept over the land and the people who welcomed it as a wind of destruction. Whether it is studied in . . . Ancient Italy, the towns of Russia, the plantations of the southern United States, or in the sugar and other plantations of Brazil, slavery is always ruin, intoxication, death. For a time it succeeds in covering, with the metallic brillance of its tiny nucleus, the darkness on all sides; but, when the moment of combustion has gone, it is evident that the luminosity was but an insignificant point compared to the mass, opaque, deserted and without life, of the whole system."

Joaquim Nabuco, *O Abolicionismo*, 1882

Nineteenth-century Brazil provides a classic example of how a colonial heritage of export-oriented agriculture based on slave manpower shaped the patterns of economic and social change in the post-colonial period and formed a neo-colonial structure with predictable and inevitable social consequences.

Brazil's relatively peaceful transition from colony to independent monarchy caused no loss in human and capital resources. But in order to expand its role in the world economy, early nineteenth-century Brazil required two elements: a profitable export commodity in which it might enjoy comparative advantage, and manpower. The solution of these problems explains the permanence of monarchy in Brazil as a political framework for nineteenth-century development and justifies the complaint after the empire's collapse in 1889 that Brazil was still "essentially agricultural" and a "trading post" on the Atlantic coast for the developed nations of the world.

Before 1830 Brazil had entered the world economy through the export of a series of commodities, first dyewood, then sugar, and between 1690 and 1770, gold and diamonds. Dyewood export on a large scale ended by 1600, mining operations declined drastically after 1770, while sugar exports and cotton proved uncompetitive after about 1800. The relative stagnation of the Brazilian economy in the first decades of the nineteenth century coincided with attacks upon the slave trade and projects for gradual emancipation of slaves, who then numbered roughly two million, or two-thirds of the population in 1820. Early attempts to diversify through industrial projects failed almost immediately; Brazil lacked trained workers, technology, transport facilities, and for obvious reasons sustained demand. More to the point, by the commercial treaty of 1810, which was in reality a "privilege-creating instrument," England continued the dominant role in the Brazilian economy which she had formerly exercised through her economic satellite, Portugal. English cotton textiles and iron and steel products poured into Brazil, undermining any possibility of such import-substitution, despite Brazil's favorable resource endowment.

What preserved and expanded the Brazilian way of life was the development of a new export commodity, coffee. Soil and climatic conditions were favorable; proximity to ports reduced the factor of transport costs by muleback; and external demand proved elastic, particularly in the United States. Within three decades, the mobilization of land and labor factors permitted coffee exports to constitute 40 per cent of total exports by value. The political influence of coffee planters led to the rapid formation of coffee estates on virgin land with available slave labor. Initial capital outlays on primitive equipment were minimal. The major bottle-neck to sustained and expanded production, however, was manpower, and in the Brazilian socio-economic colonial heritage, the only pool of available manpower was in the African slave trade.

Up to about 1800, Brazilian manpower requirements had brought approximately 2.25 million Negroes from the western and eastern coasts of black Africa. In the next fifty years, to supply northeastern sugar estates and especially the expanding coffee estates near Rio de Janeiro, 1.35 million more Negroes were imported, roughly 38 per cent of all slaves imported between 1600 and 1850. In fact, over 370,000 were imported in the last decade of the slave traffic, 1840–50, with the large-scale assistance of United States shipbuilders, captains and crews, despite the intense counter-pressure of the British government and the British navy. As a study of pressure group politics, the maintenance of the African slave trade by the Brazilian planter elite against the most dominant world power of that time merits careful analysis. One measure of its effectiveness is the cold statistical record of a higher annual import rate of African chattel slaves in the decade of the 1840's than for any previous decade in Brazilian history. Only relentless British pressure via escalation of gun-boat diplomacy forced the Brazilian government to yield in 1850 and enforce prohibitions against the trade.

Almost another forty years elapsed before the final abolition of slavery in Brazil (1888) well after the institution had disappeared elsewhere in the Americas. A number of factors brought its final demise. Abolition of the African trade concentrated slaves in profitable coffee growing areas in south central Brazil where slave prices were higher than in the

sugar-growing north. By the 1880's, however, productivity of
the old coffee areas of Rio de Janeiro and southern Minas
dropped because of an aging, contracting labor force and because of soil exhaustion. Simultaneously, the development of
the extraordinarily profitable English-built and English-
operated São Paulo railroad permitted Paulista planters to
expand coffee cultivation into virgin areas by cutting transport costs. Further, from mid-century onward Paulista planters had experimented with the importation of west European immigrants to replace slaves. By 1888 almost 70 per
cent of all immigrants entering Brazil were pouring into the
São Paulo area. Largely Italian in origin, followed by Portuguese, most of these immigrants began their occupational
careers as sharecroppers on coffee plantations. Finally mass
slave desertions in São Paulo forced a reluctant government
to enact abolition without compensation, without civil war
but not without confrontation and violence.

The aftermath of abolition in Brazil as in the United
States was the twin evils of sharecropping and tenancy as
destitute freedmen returned to old quarters or sought new
employers. Former slaveowners, in turn, abandoned the
monarchy for the republic of 1889. Thus, as one Brazilian
historian has acidly observed, the founding of the Brazilian
republic in 1889 was merely the transition from coffee with
slaves to coffee with free labor. Immigrant manpower made
possible the extraordinary expansion of coffee cultivation in
São Paulo down to the crisis of 1929 and the preservation of
Brazil's export-oriented economy.

8

"The time will come when we Mexicans will require nothing, when we will have achieved perhaps a higher level of prosperity and power than England; but that time has not yet arrived, and now we need England's money, credit and influence."

El Sol, 1825

"English capital has done what English armies could not do. Today our country is tributary to England . . . the gold that the English capitalists take out of Argentina or carry off in the form of products does us no more good than the Irish get from the revenues that the English lords take out of Ireland."

Juan B. Justo, 1896

Paralleling the economic expansion of the Latin American export sector were modifications—more apparent than real —in colonial trade patterns. The Iberian system of trade and navigation collapsed with the outbreak of conflict after 1810, and the achievement of independence implemented one of the widespread aspirations of the last decades under Iberian colonialism, free or direct trade, that is, commercial liberty. The major ports of the ex-colonies in the Gulf of Mexico and along the shores of the South Atlantic and Pacific oceans now received ships directly from the North Atlantic economic centers. Since customs duties which raised the cost of imports appreciably remained the major source of revenue for the ex-colonial governments, the volume of contraband especially in English goods long remained high. English merchant firms soon predominated in Spanish American and Brazilian ports since French restorationist governments refused to recognize the independence of Spain's American colonies. There is reason to believe the French hoped that eventual Spanish reconquest of the colonies with French backing would lead to French commercial penetration on a privileged basis. France's political conservatism was to prove costly to French manufacturers and exporters. By the 1830's, however, French firms and those of the United States and Switzerland appeared in Latin America. As a bloc the foreign merchants represented what the newly liberated criollo elite considered superior and more enlightened cultures; they provided long isolated criollos a demonstration effect in their standard of living, dress, household furnishings, cuisine, in over-all life-style. The rich travel literature of the early nineteenth century testifies to the foreigner's sense of superiority mixed with bemusement at the strange traditions, customs, institutions, and attitudes of the newly liberated Latin American nations. In the criollos' haste to imitate the external forms of the new merchants' way of life one detects a sense of backwardness and inferiority; the deference once accorded the peninsulars was transferred to other west Europeans and to the North Americans.

In one respect, however, one fear of Spanish and Portuguese merchant oligopolists during the last colonial decades did fail to materialize. English, French, and United States merchants could not completely dominate the national economies of Latin America down to the retail level. Instead, at the wholesale level a division or specialization developed according to the origin of imports, and allowed Iberians to share foreign trade with the newcomers. Iberians were reduced to their traditional products, wines and food specialties; the French concentrated on products destined for consumption by high income groups, wines and liqueurs, fine textiles, glassware, jewelry, and furniture. Predictably enough, the English controlled the lion's share of imports of iron and steel equipment, hardware and especially cotton and woolen textiles. Unlike the French, the English concentrated on sales of relatively mass consumption goods stressing uniform quality and low prices. By the middle of the century, the circle of large-scale importers had been widened but—as in the colonial past—foreigners effectively dominated the supply and price of imports and exports and exchange flows.

Moreover, urban and rural retail trade remained in Spanish or Portuguese hands because of linguistic advantage, superior knowledge of domestic patterns of distribution and greater readiness to accept the rigors of life in the interior. Non-Iberian wholesalers sold to Iberian middlemen who, in turn, supplied the retailers of the cities, the commission agents or factors of estate owners, and pack-peddlers and shopkeepers of the interior. In this sense Spaniards and Portuguese preserved the infrastructure inherited from colonial times. A small number of wealthy Iberian merchants maintained age-old patterns of recruitment. From the peninsula came young men often nephews, to learn their trade in America, to "make America" as they always had. Their apprenticeship consisted of long hours of work from sun-up to late evening, close supervision by the *patrón*, secrecy of operations, postponement of consumption. Salaries were kept by the patrón for investment in the firm and, unless a clerk married into the patrón's family, he received back pay and interest at a specified date and was assisted in establishing his own firm.

The pattern of long apprenticeship was maintained primarily because the reward of dedicated service could be large. In the nineteenth century the merchant in Latin America achieved a status greater even than in colonial times. Partly because of his wealth, his frequent loans to insolvent governments, his political influence and close association with the landholding elite, he emerged a highly prestigious figure of society. Foreign merchants were particularly prestigious because their home governments often remonstrated forcefully when their interests were affected by governmental policy; none were more so than the English merchants resident in the major cities of Latin America.

It is by now obvious that those who profited most in the eighteenth century from west European colonialism in the New World were the English merchants and manufacturers, bankers and shippers. Their greatest harvest came in the nineteenth century when they enjoyed a dominant position in the trade of the area. The backwardness of the Iberian metropolises in capital and technology opened the way to English entrepreneurs. Their textiles and hardware undersold those of their competitors; their capital resources facilitated long-term operations including the payment of high import duties; they extended credits to Latin American merchants at half the interest rates of their competitors; their shipping supplied more than 50 per cent of the volume of imports; London was the financial center which handled international payments to the exporters of France, Germany, and the United States, who, in turn, sold to Latin America.

After mid-century English economic influence mushroomed in Latin America. English investment increased at a rapid rate and flowed into railroads, urban utilities, and government securities. By lowering transportation costs through railroad construction in Mexico, Argentina, and Brazil, the English stimulated their own capital goods industry and the export possibilities of Latin American plantations, ranches, mines. Indeed, one suspects that by the 1840's English merchants recognized that the limits of Latin American demand had been attained and that the problem was to increase sales by the development of unused or poorly used resources in the interior through railroad construction.

Toward the end of the century when ports and capital cities of Latin America burgeoned into commercial, financial, and distributive hubs for the developing hinterland, the English expanded their role in the national economies of the area by supplying the technical advice, equipment, maintenance, and—above all—the investment capital for urbanization: for port works and docks, street-lighting, sewage and water systems, and urban transport. The English had been the major factor in the destruction of Iberian imperialism; on its ruins they erected the informal imperialism of free trade and investment.

CHAPTER VI

Politics and Society

"Scarcely had the revolution of independence ended when, as a natural result of the laws of society, the reaction of the colonial spirit and of the interests which that revolution had defeated began to appear. The leaders who had served that revolution carried that spirit in their training and in their hearts."

J. V. Lastarria, *Recuerdos literarios,* 1885

"It must be said that, despite the successful revolution whose beginnings I have witnessed and which permits high hopes for the future of the Brazilians, very great changes have not been able to occur in the interior of their country. The elements of rapid reform are lacking in countries whose population is low and where ignorance is so widespread."

A. de Saint-Hilaire, *Voyage dans les provinces de Rio de Janeiro et de Minas Geraes,* about 1822

Revolution provides historians with the most convenient benchmark for measuring change over time. The temporary shattering of social stability and the monopoly of force, the replacement of one segment of an elite by another or of one class by another, the involvement of large groups in violence in the cities or in warfare in the countryside to precipitate change, the creation of new instruments of governance, and, above all, the opportunity for latent social and economic conflict to burst out into public debate in constituent assemblies and in polemical pamphleteering—these aspects of the revolutionary process draw analysts to emphasize the newness of the post-revolutionary era, the so-called breakthroughs.

Before the twentieth century the great moments in the history of Latin America are the conquest decades of the early

sixteenth century and, almost three centuries later, the up-
heavals which broke the colonial mold and ushered in the
era of "national" histories. In examining the formation of
sovereign states stripped of imperial constraints and subordination and capable of independent action, historians understandably tend at first to emphasize discontinuities, innovation, change. By contrast with the superficial immobilism of
the colonial years the variety of conflict in nineteenth-
century Latin America suggests that the colonial mold had
indeed been shattered. Certainly the mere listing of cross-
currents supports this view: the schism between Liberals and
Conservatives; clericalism and anti-clericalism or to use a
different terminology, ultramontanism and gallicanism,
philosophical radicalism and traditionalism; the assimilation
of positivism and social Darwinism. These materials have
often been incorporated by historians into a chronological
and topical framework: following independence, a search
for a principle of authority when the old superstructure of
obedience to the Iberian metropolises and their colonial representatives collapsed; then the resurgence of conservatism
enshrined in the constitutions of centralizing political systems; the ascendance of Liberalism undermining the
Bourbon-like politics of restoration; and, finally, after about
1870, the waning of internal war and the apparent conciliation of Liberal-Conservative ideological differences in some
sort of compromise.

Yet within the variety of nineteenth-century historical experience one detects large outcroppings of the colonial heritage, symptoms of its survival under favorable conditions:
the wide, discretionary powers granted to the chief executive
over legislative and judicial bodies; the enclaves of privilege
in the form of separate ecclesiastical and military jurisdic-

tions, the "corporative spirit"; municipal and regional ad-
ministrations endowed with political jurisdiction but in fact
suffering political anemia; regional nuclei of power in the
form of local magnates sharing authority and patronage,
alliance and kinship, aggregating clients and dependents;
public office used as a means of dispensing public wealth to
dependents near and distant, associated with widespread
graft as a substitute for administrative efficiency—and this
list is by no means comprehensive. In probing the contradiction between discontinuity in political structure and process
on the one hand and inescapable continuities on the other,
the historian must therefore question the validity of the wars
of independence as an historical benchmark. If one starts
with the hypothesis that the criollo component of the Iberian
elite group of colonial times consolidated and dominated the
independence movement, then the contradiction may be resolved. In this light the benchmark indicates merely that the
criollos' principal aspiration was achieved: substitution of
Iberian dominance and preservation of the colonial heritage
of political and social structures. Post-independence criollos
to survive had to constrain social change, to prevent the independence movement from turning into a continuing revolution.

Thus the major problem confronting the criollo upper
class in the first decades of independence was the consolidation of colonial patterns of political elitism and social stratification so as to contain social tensions in the middle and
lower strata of colonial society. Within the new polity of republic or as in Brazil, constitutional monarchy, acceptable
mechanisms had to be inserted to preserve a directing class
of criollos, to incorporate potentially explosive middle
groups of Whites, mulattoes, mestizos, castas, and freedmen,

and, finally, to render politically passive the labor force of Latin America's agrarian economies—illiterate Amerinds and Negroes.

The policy of political and social containment concerned, therefore, two major groups, the largest of which was the rural labor force. During the colonial period the upper strata of Iberians and criollos invariably coalesced in the face of Amerindian or Negro revolts, whether in the form of explosive rural peasant revolts or in destructive urban riots, both of which flared up periodically. Invariably, too, these threats to the established order—slave insurrections, Amerindian revolts against such injustice as personal service, forced labor, loss of communal property to encroaching haciendas, inflexible tribute payment—were quelled by ruthless application of force, summary trial, and public punishment of leaders. In the nineteenth century the pattern of repression was maintained. Fear of rebellion understandably led criollos seeking first autonomy, then independence, to reduce appeals to Amerinds or Negroes wherever possible. But where the vicissitudes of the struggle for independence forced criollos to appeal in desperation to the lowest classes —to promise ultimate emancipation to slaves and to Amerinds full equality in the new society—afterward the new political elites were quick to reduce, even eliminate, this commitment to change.

In such circumstances the criollo weapon against the metropolitan overlord—the eighteenth-century concept of a glorious Amerindian pre-conquest civilization in Mexico and Peru shared by those born in America, no matter their racial background—proved a two-edged weapon. It legitimized both the Amerindian quest for equity and the criollo aspiration for monopoly of the political process, since both groups shared an identity of birthplace with the now distinguished pre-conquest rulers of the continent. In the twentieth century, indigenismo or Indianism proved a powerful bond in the forging of nationalism, in the incorporation of isolated Amerindian elements; but in the 1820's it loomed as a threat to criollo monopolization of political power.

The criollo tactic which followed from the inherent promise of equality of citizenship in the new polity, was to legislate out of existence wherever possible what were considered holdovers of the colonial regime of protected enclaves of privilege. Indians would now be able to divide their communally owned lands and to dispose of them at will; they would have no special taxes or courts; in theory they would participate as citizens with full political rights and responsibilities. No longer would there be Indians and non-Indians, but only rich and poor. Laudable objectives, but to Indian communities this equality threatened the mechanisms that protected them against the skills of those better prepared for the competitive individualism of a Liberal economy and polity. Those reared in the tradition of "enclave" polities were ill-prepared for juridical equality. Amerinds who abandoned their communities were incorporated as wage laborers; as illiterates or domestics, they were conveniently disenfranchised by the new constitutions. Those who remained in their communities sought protection in further isolation, or reacted in hopeless revolt. In Mexico and Peru intermittent criollo-Indian warfare continued throughout the nineteenth century. Here and elsewhere the rural masses sought redress by supporting local magnates, usually landlords—the caciques or caudillos—who promised protection against the central government in return for local allegiance and fidelity. In any event, the political participation of Amerinds was minimized.

Pacification of the second element of the work force in Latin America, the Negro in plantation agriculture, was achieved perhaps more rapidly. In Brazil, Cuba, and Venezuela fear of the contagion of the Saint Domingue or Haitian example of slave upheaval and violent anti-criollo conflict was inescapable. This fear combined with determination to maintain the African slave trade, which England opposed, accounts in large part for Cuba's loyalty to Spain and Brazil's peaceful disassociation from Portugal. In Venezuela the prolonged and violent character of the wars of independence forced both sides in the conflict to turn to slaves for military recruitment; in the process the bonds of slavery were loosened. However, between 1821 and 1830 a variety of mechanisms were adopted which delayed emancipation until 1854: children born to slave mothers after 1821 were free but ultimately forced to work for their masters until age twenty-five; other slaves could be manumitted for compensation, but this fund was never adequate; local authorities meanwhile were given broad powers to enforce legal sanctions on forced labor.

In Cuba the massive inflow of slaves of varied African provenience from the 1790's onward introduced a labor force ill-prepared for co-ordinated rebellion. At the same time maintenance of the tie to imperial Spain ensured the continuation of the slave trade and of slavery itself. Similarly dependence upon Negro slave labor led Brazilian plantation owners to seek refuge within the Portuguese imperial system. Then, when English pressure forced the Portuguese government to abandon the trade, Brazil turned to independence in defense of its access to African manpower. Not until 1850 did the Brazilian monarchy yield to English naval and diplomatic pressure to end the trade. Moreover the diffused nature of slavery throughout Brazil strengthened the power of planters who in the 1820's crushed proposals to end the trade and to institute a program of gradual emancipation. The Cuban and Brazilian experience suggests that the persistence of slavery in Cuba is associated with continued Spanish colonialism and in Brazil with the perpetuation of centralized control under monarchy.

At the same time perpetuation of a sharp two-class system in the countryside and the failure to resolve social tensions led to the full emergence of a political element which had been latent in the colonial regime: the rural political leader, the Venezuelan *caudillo* or the Brazilian *coronel* with whom central governments, republican or monarchical, had to come to terms. Caudillo, cacique, coronel—these significant elements of rural nineteenth-century Latin America indicate the persistence, indeed the new vigor, of colonial patterns of socio-economic and political control. For most rural Latin Americans, these local figures functioned as the real government, legitimized by the political system, respected by national governments and their local representatives in the judicial, administrative, and military bureaucracy.

The most potentially troublesome of the neo-colonial political elements to be harnessed to the criollos' new polity were the colonial interstitial groups: mestizos, mulattoes, and castas in general, and the poor Whites. The last-named had represented in the colonial era the major component of free immigration, usually as tradesmen, artisans, or soldiery. After 1810 this current diminished sharply although the inflow resumed in post-independence years. Their white color, their skills as profit-oriented petty tradesmen, artisans, estate foremen, non-commissioned or commissioned officers facilitated their relatively rapid absorption by the criollo leadership.

Mestizos, mulattoes, and castas were not so readily absorbed, however. It has been pointed out that at the end of the eighteenth century their skills and sometimes their educational background created aspirations to achieve status commensurate with their talents and to destroy barriers of color legitimized and enforced by the colonial system. Negro freedmen and free-born mulattoes, Indians who abandoned their communities to become culturally "Europeanized," and the free floating mestizos—these tended to abandon their rural homes and ties to seek employment and mobility in the cities. There they were attracted by the appeals of the criollo Liberals who emphasized the open society, political participation, democratic ideals. Active participation in independence movements as common soldiers, officers, guerrilla leaders, as pamphleteers and journalists—in sum as valued co-participants—made it difficult in the 1820's to ignore their demands. All the more so since unlike Indian peons and Negro slaves, they accepted the values of the criollo class: individualism, competition, wealth-accumulation. And their numbers grew more rapidly than those of Indian peons or Negro slaves. Unless they could be incorporated, there always existed the possibility that they—perhaps the group most alienated from the *ancien régime,* oscillating between rejection of and absorption into the criollos' order—might turn to the submerged orders to destroy the criollos' dream of consolidating the old regime with the fewest possible concessions to the lower classes.

These were the elements that the criollo leaders who inherited the movement of independence had to aggregate in a stable polity as they sought to create appropriate constitutional forms to preserve their own leadership, to incorporate the most assimilable elements of other classes, to legislate, as it were, the conditions of political and economic, if not social, progress. In assaying the outcome and the significance of their efforts it may now be useful to sketch out the major political groups of the Iberian world before and after the independence of the Ibero-American colonies, to indicate the political models then available, and to suggest points of continuity between colony and nationhood.

Around 1800 three major elite groups of varying political influence existed in the Iberian metropolitan and colonial world. First, the *traditionalists*—peninsulares for the most part—who sought security by clinging to time-worn institutions and attitudes. Next, those properly called their allies, who were equally dedicated to the preservation of traditional society and its values, but who recognized that tradition could be preserved only by making certain inescapable adjustments to the structure of society and politics, modifying the parts to maintain the whole. These might be categorized as *realists*—often military men, higher bureaucrats, or noblemen—who saw the peril in isolating themselves from reality in Europe and, more to the point, in America. There was a third group, of greater influence in America perhaps than on the Iberian peninsula, consisting of wealthy landowners, miners, merchants, churchmen, and bureaucrats whose full development necessitated far more profound socio-political changes than the realists would accept. This group was the *insurgent* spearhead during the struggle for independence and in the civil wars during post-independence decades. This group, unlike the traditionalists and realists, would if necessary and did in fact seek support of the mestizo and mulatto groups for the attainment of its ends.

From the crucible of independence there emerged two principal political configurations, *Conservatives* who attracted the former traditionalists and realists now accepting independence, plus those insurgents now intent on preserving old economic and social structures, and *Liberals* who aggregated both radicals and moderates from among the old realists and insurgents. To these groups fell the responsibility for the creation of independent nations. What were the external models to be chosen and adapted to the new circumstances?

Two groups of models were available to the organizers of new polities in Latin America after 1824. First were pre-revolutionary France with its enlightened despotism, administrative efficiency, stratified society, and enclaves of privilege, and England where constitutional government fused hereditary monarchy and political representation in elected bodies for the most influential socio-economic groups or classes. England was economically progressive and politically conservative, qualities which permitted her to survive the war with France without serious reform. The second group, in contrast, represented the products of revolutionary circumstances: the United States after 1789 and France after 1815. The United States offered an impressive example of a once-colonial area which forged a political structure combining the necessities of territorial unity and regional autonomy, elected executive and legislative bodies, and incorporating within a republican framework all residents, citizens and non-citizens, free men and slaves. As for France of the post-1815 restoration, it had great influence in Brazil since it accepted features of the Revolution in the Napoleonic codes and integrated the bourgeoisie into a stratified social system reminiscent of the old regime, while a strong monarch checked the representative bodies picked by a restricted electorate of property holders.

Whatever group the newly independent nations chose to follow, all rejected Iberian models of political structures: the absolutism of Spain and Portugal. After independence there was in the minds of the Latin American political elite too intimate an identification between colonialism and absolutism, between backwardness and unrepresentative government. Moreover the restoration of absolutism in Spain and Portugal led to civil war there, the appearance of pretorian politics, and the notable absence of any effective modernization. For many of the elite of post-independence Latin America, the Pyrenees were the southern frontier of modernizing western Europe.

The option before the creole elite in the 1820's was, therefore, between constitutional monarchy and republicanism. Social overtones of the struggles for independence were muted, and there was no problem in restricting the suffrage drastically, or for that matter, maintaining slavery within republican institutions. Republics are not necessarily democracies. On the other hand, the constitutional framework had to permit the participation of numerically small but articulate bourgeois and middle-class elements which neo-colonial Latin American growth required. They became vital to the Latin American economy of the nineteenth century, filling the regional and national bureaucracies, participating in commercial and financial enterprises, playing indispensable roles in journalism and politics. Many of these groups were the spearheads of Liberalism, first trusting to federal political structures to introduce changes, later turning to republican authoritarianism to impose them. At the end of the

nineteenth century increased economic opportunity permitted their absorption by the elite they had once vehemently
attacked and they became Liberal autocrats who rationalized
the existence of a Liberal aristocracy or directing class which
wholeheartedly accepted the tenets of laisser-faire.

It must be remembered that at the beginning of the struggle for independence in Latin America the creole elite as a
group preferred monarchical institutions, provided economic policy was modified. The frequency with which various areas of Latin America during the anti-colonial struggle
flirted with the idea of monarchy—and even created monarchical regimes afterward in Mexico and Brazil—leads to
the conclusion that in the 1820's the creole elite still preferred constitutional monarchy. It is quite plausible to pro-
pose that had the Spanish government accepted in 1783 the
recommendations of the Bourbon realist, Aranda, that the
Spanish Bourbons create monarchies in Mexico and Peru
linked by dynastic ties and annual tribute payments to
Spain, monarchy in Latin America during the nineteenth
century would have been the predominant form of political
organization. In fact, monarchy was tried and collapsed
twice in Mexico, 1822-23 and 1864-67; in Brazil; however,
the presence of the Portuguese royal family as refugees after
1807 facilitated the survival of monarchy until to 1889.

While monarchy was frequently contemplated in Latin
America, most of the emergent nations chose republican
structures. Internal conflict was not resolved, however, by
agreement on a republic. There still remained crucial issues:
what kind of a republic, federal (decentralized) or unitary
(centralized), presidential or parliamentary, popular or elitist, democratic or aristocratic, Liberal or Conservative? The
cleavages represented more than differences over form. In a

very real sense conflict over political structures mirrored
sharp differences over the existing and future structure of society, over access to and distribution of power, over the
course of economic change. At stake was the issue of who
would inherit the revolution. Liberals as a group intended to
believe in a secular state, without an established politicized
Roman Catholic church; in an enlarged electorate of minimal qualifications for voters and direct rather than indirect
elections; in state-supported educational systems; in the
elimination of holdovers of colonial institutions—military
and ecclesiastical courts of wide jurisdiction, the display of
titles and emblems of nobility, entailed estates. A few Liberals tried to model their political structure according to what
they found in the constitution of the United States, particularly decentralization (federalism), which they considered
responsible for that country's remarkable progress. They
were quite aware that the United States constitution brought
together political entities which had once enjoyed great autonomy under colonial rule whereas in Spanish American
republics, federalism or regional autonomy contradicted the
imperial structures. What was essential was the fact that
federative political structures promised to meet sectional demands for autonomy in economic affairs, permitting the region to maximize local resources, human and natural, for
local benefit. This had been a key factor leading outlying regions to support the capital cities in the struggle for independence.

One should not exaggerate the unity of Liberals or for
that matter of Conservatives. Some Liberals (*exaltados*)
wished to push forward to the achievement of Utopia
quickly; others (*moderados*) more wary, or perhaps more
realistic, certainly more gradualist, shared such aspirations

but preferred to enact reformist legislation piecemeal, partly because they were not fully committed to a democratic society in the near future, partly because they feared to antagonize the Conservative opposition into violence. For their part Conservatives were not all unreconstructed or committed to the preservation of as much as possible of the colonial structures minus Spanish overlordship. Some Conservatives welcomed economic change, even industrialization and a proletariat, if only to absorb the growing number of unemployed artisans and their families. Other Conservatives logically embraced federalism when they no longer held a majority in the congress or failed to control the executive office and therefore found in regional autonomy protection against Liberals in power.

Viewed as a whole, post-independent political structures, whether Liberal-Conservative republics or a monarchy as in Brazil, shared basic elements by 1850: strong executives with wide discretionary powers such as the power to declare unilaterally a state of siege; national governments authorized to appoint provincial or state executives (whether they were termed presidents, governors, or intendents), and capable of controlling local elections via extensive police and judicial powers; and voting qualifications which required high income and excluded rural and urban wage-earners, domestics, and even in some cases commercial employees. Both types of government systematically excluded the propertyless, impoverished free citizens from political participation while indirect elections likewise filtered the elements of popular voting. A generous estimate of the political participation of the male population in all Latin American nations would probably approach 2 to 4 per cent during most of the nineteenth century. In Brazil, in 1881, some 142,000 voted out of a population of about 15 million. Unlike the United States, Brazil did not even accord slaves partial counting in determining regional representation in the parliament. It should be recalled that the absence of primary schools effectively filtered the electorate by keeping literacy rates low: by about 1865 one child per three inhabitants in some states of the United States was in primary school; in the province of Buenos Aires where educational opportunities were superior to those of the rest of the Argentine republic, the ratio was one to twenty-five.

Perhaps the most notable political change in the nineteenth century was the decline in the incidence of sectional revolts after about 1850. One suspects that it was less due to constitutional provisions than to the realization by sectional elites that national economic growth would be uneven, that only certain sections could hope to profit by response to external demand, capital inflows, and technology, and that it behooved the elite of backward or declining sections to move to the capital cities where opportunities in business, government bureaucracy, and politics were greater. There they merged with their counterparts in what was called conciliation or compromise. Small wonder, then, that by 1890 or roughly seven decades after independence the ex-Iberian colonies had everywhere created republican structures of government which were by no means democratizing, much less democratic. They were oligarchic republics, sometimes federative in theory, but centralized in fact. The descendants of the criollo elite of 1810 or of those who had been absorbed by that elite afterward occupied key positions in all sectors of government: legislative, judicial, and executive, the naval forces and to almost the same degree, the army. These elites, by a felicitous combination of force, shrewdly drafted constitutions, and skillful co-optation of the more capable of the lower orders had indeed creamed off the revolutions of independence.

The underlying stability of the basic institutions of nineteenth-century Latin America does not contradict the observation that politics there was volatile, unpredictable, and disruptive. Rather, such conflict expressed factionalism among the elite, an outgrowth of the colonial heritage of regional oligarchies and family interests. We must realize that given the structure of society, the nature of paternalistic relations between landowners and dependents, and the structure of politics, violence involved small numbers of participants in local areas while the general machinery of government was untouched. No example of violence consumed so many lives, devastated so large an area and destroyed so much property as civil war in the United States a century ago. In major Latin American nations—in Argentina, Mexico, Brazil, and Chile—with few exceptions chief executives filled out their terms of office or left them alive after 1850. In the nineteenth century, no major Latin American republic equaled the record of the United States in the incidence of presidential assassinations. In sum, in Latin America the colonial heritages reinforced by external and internal factors produced economic growth without appreciable sociopolitical change during the nineteenth century. This was the situation about 1890 and it was not materially modified with the exception of Mexico until the coming of the Great Depression in 1929.

2

"Aryan civilization is represented in Brazil by a tiny minority of the white race to which has fallen the burden of defending it, not only against the anti-social acts—or crimes—of its own representatives, but also against the anti-social acts of inferior races, whether they are true crimes in the view of the races, or whether on the contrary they are manifestations of the conflict, the struggle for existence between the superior civilization of the white race and vague signs of civilization of the conquered or subdued races."

Nina Rodrigues, *As raças humanas,* 1894

"The white [in Mexico] is proprietor; the Indian, proletariat. The white is rich; the Indian, poor, wretched. The descendants of Spaniards are au courant of the advances of the century, and of all scientific discoveries; the Indian is entirely unaware of them. . . . The white lives in a magnificent town house; the Indian is isolated in the countryside and lives in a miserable shack . . . two different people in one land; what is worse, two people to a certain degree enemies."

F. Pimentel, about 1865

Social stability, it is now evident, was a principal characteristic of the history of Latin America in the nineteenth century as it continued to be well into the twentieth century. For decades after independence the few dominant families—patriarchal, extended social webs of wealth, education, power, prestige—intermarried, produced children, sent sons to the handful of select secondary schools in the national capitals, then (especially after 1850) into one of the national faculties of law, medicine, engineering of the one national university, ultimately niched them into careers in law and politics, finance or medicine, or agricultural or ranching enterprise, and enrolled them in the few select and color-conscious social clubs, and in just about this order. Then sons married first, second, or third cousins who constituted practically the only elements of their peer group, and the cycle of elite perpetuation and stratification continued.

Social rigidity and exclusivism dominated but not entirely so. The elite did make room at the top for select capable White newcomers as had the colonial elite. These filtered into the landholding groups from the commercial and financial elements required by a slowly expanding export agriculture extending its linkages back into interior provinces and across the Atlantic to economic centers at Paris, London, and Hamburg. The landholding aristocracy monopolized the ranks of the upper bureaucracy, legal professions, and the executive, legislative, and judicial organs of government. When national capitals multiplied their functions as administrative, commercial, financial, and distributive hubs, they attracted from abroad the first wave of nineteenth-century immigrants, educated White elements equipped with skills and overseas connections in short supply locally: merchants, doctors, engineers, educators.

Largest in number were the merchants. To be sure, Iberian merchants had predominated among colonial immigrants; despite their accumulation of wealth and influence colonial merchants nonetheless did not hold what colonial society judged the most prestigious occupation. Fulfillment of one of the aspirations of independence, unlimited commercial contact with the outside world, gave to the merchant in nineteenth-century Latin America full membership on his own terms, as one who played a key role in developing economies and societies. Moreover, unlike the colonial merchants who often had a minimal education acquired in underdeveloped Spain or Portugal, nineteenth-century merchants represented what seemed advanced, modern, and "civilized" European centers; through their mediation, the technology and civilization of the "West" entered Latin America. These essential White immigrants from France, England, Switzerland, Germany, and Italy proved as eligible and acceptable for marriage alliances with criollo landowning families as the Iberians in the colonial and neo-colonial eras.

The elite recruited a few members from a second social segment as well, low-income Whites in medicine, law, or the military. They were the products of the few educational establishments or training schools established after independence to furnish cadres once found largely if not exclusively in the Iberian metropolises.

Education and income also smoothed the path of upward mobility for the suitably "whitened" mestizos and mulattoes whose numbers were significant everywhere in Iberian America at the end of the colonial period. Education—as even the percentage of the school-age population of modern Latin America indicates today—was in general a restricted privilege, not a common right. It was and is a measure of social constraint, a highly selective barrier to income and status. In most Latin American countries then as now, the most effective means of ensuring rigid social stratification was curtailment of primary education, and with few exceptions (Argentina, Chile) budgetary allocations were reduced to the minimum consistent to maintain the competence of the political, social, and economic elite. One need only contrast the share of budgetary outlays on armed forces and primary education to understand why social tension in Latin

America was long considered a matter for the police or the national armed forces.

One might ask if the neglect of public education indicates a lack of responsibility on the part of the neo-colonial elite toward the masses, a consciously created blindness to the interrelationship between the improvement of all citizens or inhabitants and the possibility of general improvement of society as a whole. No doubt the elitist nature of neo-colonial education was part of the colonial heritage, but this is perhaps only begging the question. The socio-psychological complex of both colonial and neo-colonial upper classes mirrored the attitude of the superior White or near-White lords to the dependent population which colonial legal terminology had called people without reason, *gente sin razón,* for whom natural law prescribed the status of inferiors. Dependents were not full citizens of the nation. In neo-colonial Latin America they were quasi-wards requiring leadership, not education. Moreover the technological requirements of export economies were not high in the nineteenth century; literacy was not a prerequisite for the man with the hoe.

For Indians and most mestizos socio-economic disadvantages represented great barriers to mobility. In southernmost Latin America Indians were literally eliminated or absorbed into the work force. In other areas, the expansion of estate farming and ranching reinforced Amerinds' effort to preserve themselves via their colonial defense mechanism, their community. Their contribution to national output above subsistence remained minimal. Fear of the White man, and an even greater fear of the White man's "emissary"—the biological or cultural mestizo, the Indian who dressed, ate, acted like a White man but was more dangerous because he was a sort of cultural broker between two worlds—led them to buttress the bonds of community; when pushed beyond the limits of almost infinite toleration, they broke into revolts which, as in the colonial era, were ruthlessly suppressed. They were increasingly isolated from the White man's world, visited by a few traders, receiving only occasional attention from the White curate.

Other Amerindian communities formed a biological pool, as it were, breeding human beings to be drained off to meet the labor demands of growing export economies. Sometimes, following peasant rebellions, they were simply resettled en masse as when the Mexican Yaqui were shipped off to labor in the distant henequen plantations of Yucatan. More important, the spread of smallpox vaccination probably was a factor in their demographic growth; as population pressed upon scarce resources, the young drifted off to railroad construction, to estates, to small towns, and ultimately to the large capital cities where they entered the underworld of the culture of poverty.

The White man's world was indeed broad and alien, but the Indian or mestizo, at least in the areas of pre-conquest civilizations, still carried in his rags the faint aura of former greatness, which engendered respect in some intellectual quarters. Toward the end of the century indigenista nationalism recognized the wretched marginal man that conquest, colonialism, and neo-colonialism had made of once-skilled Amerinds. If he was now only a caricature of his past dignity, there were the cities constructed in pre-conquest times, the imposing religious edifices, the extraordinary objects of gold metallurgy, featherwork, and textiles which the Iberian conquerors of the sixteenth century had proudly shipped to the metropolis to buttress their tales of prowess in overcoming skilled, organized peoples on the Western continent, and which had once evoked the unrestrained admiration of Albrecht Dürer. The objects were displayed, if not at home then in the museums of Vienna, Berlin, and Paris where even traveling Latin American criollo aristocrats could admire them. Pre-conquest cultures provided an intellectual bond between masters and dependents: Whites and near-Whites on the one hand, and Amerinds and mestizos on the other despite the fact that the gap between countryside and cities, between Amerindian communities and cosmopolitan nuclei was widening rapidly after about 1880. This may suggest why Mexico, for example, had a full-blooded Zapotec Indian—Benito Juárez—and an obvious if often bepowdered mestizo Porfirio Díaz as respected presidents for about four of the roughly five decades between 1857 and 1910. As we shall see, however, this is not to underestimate the racial pessimism directed toward the Amerind as well as the Negro at the end of the century.

The Negro's socio-economic handicap was far greater. The rationalization of the slave trade and chattel slavery on plantations and mines remained in neo-colonial Ibero-America: that slave traders and slaveowners had rescued him from barbarism—the myth of the Negro past. Stripped of his culture, ripped from family and community, deprived of wife or women, turned into a "human instrument of labor," the Negro carried with him everywhere in Latin America the stigma of his history, which was presumed to be no-history in one sense and chattel slavery in another. Yet, in one of the curious contradictions of history, the Negro brought to the New World as laborer in the field, as house-servant, as stevedore in tropical port towns, as disposer of garbage, has imparted a stronger imprint on many of Euro-American societies than the Indian. The Negro, his

culture and his reactions to slavery profoundly affected not
only the White. Furthermore, close contact made miscegenation inevitable, thereby projecting the African heritage and
the trauma of slavery to succeeding generations of Americans.

The ascension of the mulatto, despite the stigma of slavery, had begun in colonial times. Many achieved prominence
in the wars of independence and as doctors, lawyers, and
members of constituent congresses in the years immediately
after. His upward mobility continued in the nineteenth century. In a sense this process in neo-colonial Brazil was only
the widening and deepening of a colonial heritage which
accepted the mulatto because of his talents, and because
colonial society and economy required such talents. Colonial
society accepted him as it did the mestizo, partly because
legal color barriers kept the upflow to tolerable or assimilable proportions; in theory, the destruction of the legal racial
barriers should have accelerated the process of Negro and
mulatto integration. But the barriers of prejudice which west
European Whites have nurtured to limit the upflow of men
of color, especially the Negro and mulatto, in the New
World continued to dam the flow in neo-colonial Latin
America.

In neo-colonial Brazil, racial prejudice directed against the
Negro and mulatto survived but occasionally was diluted by
the force of circumstance. In Brazilian or for that matter,
Cuban cities, where the mass of people were Negro or
mulatto, contact with low-income immigrants from Spain
and Portugal was frequent. The French observers of Brazil's
social scene were fond of referring to the lower-class Portuguese immigrants' "goût de la négresse." Such immigrants
generally arrived without women, and their sole female con-

tacts were black or mulatto women. They were, to be sure, hardly breaking new social ground for in colonial Brazil as in the Caribbean in the eighteenth century, the cynical had noted that life was "a paradise" for mulatto women. This was hardly a feminist point of view but it did reflect a reality of sorts. More to the point, interracial conflict was minimized in neo-colonial Brazil simply because the demands of urban manpower were so great that race conflict over job opportunities failed to develop. In the long run, poor Whites were more successful in achieving income, status, and eligible wives in an individualistic, competitive, and race-conscious society.

Among the upper strata of race-conscious Brazilian society, too, there were factors that mitigated the stigma attached to negritude. Such was the elite's control over property, wealth, income, and education that the incorporation of upper-class males' mulatto offspring posed no threat; there was no threatening upsurge of people of color. With few exceptions landowning, slaveholding families accepted the products of male philandering. They were tolerated as inferior dependents in family service. And when planter families migrated from isolated estates and towns of the interior to the few large capital cities of the coast, the colored dependents went along, some to remain in family service, others to accept employment in other urban households or as artisans, petty tradesmen and porters maintaining public buildings. The ties linking freedmen and benevolent ex-masters survived, in fact were cultivated as a form of social security. Further, where mulatto males achieved distinction in law, engineering, and commerce, and were light enough to make suitable mates for White or near-White upper-class daughters, the process of whitening was often so rapid that within three generations it was—to the unknowing observer —hard to recognize that so-and-so had what Brazilians knowingly called and *still* call a "foot in the kitchen"—a black ancestor. The Brazilians put it succinctly: "Money whitens."

The process of upward social mobility of the mestizo and the mulatto in nineteenth-century Latin America should not be overstressed. It was tolerated because irreversible, because few of the upper class envisioned massive "mongrelization" of the national elite, because they controlled higher-status employment, and because the colored lower strata of Latin American society did not pose the threat of revolution from below, a vast upheaval in the Haitian style. In Brazil Whites took a prominent—in fact predominant—role as abolitionists; one vigorous mulatto abolitionist, Patrocinio, became an ardent defender of monarchy after the princess regent signed the emancipation act of 1888; Brazil's outstanding nineteenth-century novelist, the mulatto Machado de Assis, left only the most subtle reflections on the problem of race in Brazil. This is only to suggest that, by accepting social reality, the elite absorbed the upcoming mulatto and mestizo by co-optation—another colonial practice.

Co-optation advanced slowly in the eighteenth century, may have accelerated somewhat during the independence and post-independence decades to reward elements of the Amerindian and Negro masses who distinguished themselves in military service, and may have indeed slowed down in the last quarter of the century, as the unbroken colonial heritage of racism assumed a virulent form when buttressed by "scientific" rationalization and in some areas by the annual arrival of hundreds of thousands of underdeveloped, traditional but conveniently White west Europeans.

Three interrelated factors help explain the flowering of racism or, to be more precise, racial pessimism in the late nineteenth century. First, the Latin American elite perceived that the gap between the economic performance of their countries and that of the industrial giants of western Europe and North America was widening. The number of upper-class Latin Americans sent to Europe for study or mere travel grew at the end of the century to proportions never achieved under Iberian rule; on their return to capital cities or family properties in the interior the gap between civilization and backwardness was both disturbing and unforgettable. The steamship and the telegraph augmented the flow of information, technological, economic, literary, from the advanced and modernizing centers of the North Atlantic basin: European newspapers and periodicals regularly received found their way into the interior as well as the Latin American capital cities and served as a constant reminder of the superiority of White peoples over those in the backwash of change.

In searching for the causes of backwardness, the Latin American elite conveniently pinpointed the second factor in racism, the "apathy, indolence and improvidence" of the masses. Cataloguing the deficiencies of Amerinds, Negroes, and their mixtures among themselves and with Whites, they judged that races transmitted specific cultural characteristics from generation to generation and that Latin America's backwardness or underdevelopment was inescapable because of the composition of its population. The human resource endowment was inadequate. Distinguished European scholars (or is the proper term "popularizers"?) of the latter half of the century rationalized the irresistible penetration of western European and North American ways of life. Since

dynamism, innovation, and foresight characterized the
Whites at home and in the imperialist out-thrust in Africa,
Asia and on the North American continent, a host of Europeans including Gobineau and Le Bon, Spencer and Hux-
ley, and many lesser known lights, deduced that the universal man propagated by eighteenth-century liberals was a
myth, that there existed in fact a hierarchy of races, and that
the Whites or Aryans constituted the superordinate stratum,
Amerinds, Asiatics, and Africans the subordinate stratum.
The inferiors could not withstand the Whites in the "struggle for social existence." The Europeans conceded that miscegenation among Whites and near-Whites produced in
many cases acceptable offspring; on the other hand, the
greater the racial chasm, the worse the results. To convince
the White or near-White elite of the scientific validity of
these conclusions required no great effort. The concepts of
social hierarchy and the scale of social inferiority were, as we
have seen, a deeply rooted part of the colonial heritage,
going back to the sixteenth century when colonialists and
their literary defenders cited Aristotle on natural inferiority.

The apparent reluctance of Amerinds to participate in the
White man's world in the late nineteenth century, and the
Negroes' incapacity to compete with White immigrants in
some regions even in rural employment led the elite to review the premise that it was feasible to develop with such a
labor force. They did not question the exploitative nature of
the system into which the inferiors were to be integrated;
their reluctance, apathy, irresponsibility, and unresponsive-
ness to the challenge of change could, the elite felt, only be
ascribed to innate characteristics, congenital psychic and intellectual deficiencies. So the elite continued the colonial heritage of racial discrimination, only now it was buttressed by

the sociology of capitalism and imperialism, by a framework of the stages of evolution advanced by Comte—theocratic, metaphysical, positivistic—mixed with social Darwinism propounded by Spencer to explain the survival of the whitest. In a sense, the incipient universalism of the eighteenth century was replaced by concepts of the heterogeneity and hierarchy of man in the late nineteenth. To the Latin American elite in the last quarter of that century, the only road to progress was simply to substitute local manpower by massive immigration or failing to attract it, to hope that a long process of "whitening" might bleach out racial deficiencies. The vision of progress via immigration was coupled with racial prejudice and racial pessimism, although a few devoutly believed that well-planned practical education in science and technology might modify the incapacity of the masses to change.

Epilogue

1

"There are two types of union; one, friendship and confraternity; the other, dependence and subordination."

Padre Talamantes, 1808

"For a century now our economies have been linked to the international economy and 50 per cent of our population is still stagnating in pre-capitalist conditions. . . ."

Raúl Prebisch, *Towards a Dynamic Development Policy for Latin America*, 1964

"Refusals to annex are no proof of reluctance to control."

J. Gallagher and R. Robinson,
"The Imperialism of Free Trade," 1953

On concluding a synthesis of the evolution of Latin America to the end of the nineteenth century which emphasizes the permanence of certain institutions, values, and attitudes over a long time, it is appropriate to raise the question, Is the neocolonial framework as a tool of analysis applicable to Latin American development in the twentieth century, especially in the decades since 1930 or since the end of the Second World War? To be more concrete, are not the twentieth-century phenomena of rapid demographic growth, industrialization and urbanization, extension of governmental control, and expansion of bureaucracy, and—not to be exhaustive—the role of supranational corporations in the national economy and polity, indicators of qualitative change rendering obsolete reference to the survival of neocolonialism? Since there has been change in this century, can one logically assume it has been profound enough to warrant a markedly different analytical frame of reference?

That historians should stress continuity over change should surprise no one. On the other hand, the publications of economists, political scientists, anthropologists, and sociologists who examine Latin American reality and conclude in many cases that what that area of the world requires is "structural" change, suggest that neo-colonialism as an analytical tool is still effective. No one denies that change has occurred but most analysts recognize that, at least in backward, underdeveloped, or dependent areas of the globe, the heritage of the past has shaped and is shaping current widespread poverty there.

In an area universally considered highly developed such as the United States it is accepted that its heritage has determined its present peak of development, its role as *the* current dominant world power. But there exist other elements in that heritage traceable to colonial times which—like slavery and the unrestrained quest for profit—have fostered racial bitterness and the morass of the metropolises of the United States. The tradition of urban growth which compartmentalized and separated slums and luxury residences to dampen social unrest today produces the desperation of the ghetto and ineffective governmental action. Thus the heritage of the defense of private right in property and minimal state action in the defense of public interest seems to have rendered the United States incapable of coping with the mushrooming pressures of a modern, indeed ultra-modern society and economy, rendering the present "depressingly continuous with the past." Historians' abandonment of the analytical framework of consensus for that of conflict, violence, and oppression in order to understand the nation's past may be construed as the recognition that the United States, too, has not escaped the unresolved problems of the past which plague the present.

In comparable fashion, Latin Americans are re-viewing their present and probing their past only to conclude that developments over the past seventy years and more have perpetuated neo-colonial structures impeding rather than facilitating change. This, at any rate, is the structuralists' frame of reference as they review the Latin American pattern of change since about 1890.

2

Eighty years ago the ideology of development in Latin America favored the expansion of export-oriented economies on the assumption that production and export of primary products and foodstuffs would serve as the dynamic element thereby raising per capita income, facilitating elimination of illiteracy, expansion of higher education and absorption of technology, and leading inevitably to the forging of modern societies and economies such as Latin Americans saw appearing in England, France, Germany, and the United States, the "core" nation-states of the world. Relative political stability and economic change in the decades after 1850 seemed to confirm this ideology. In fact the basis of the ideology appeared sound as the volume and value of Latin America's foreign trade expanded, as railroads, ports, and communications materialized, and as a national bourgeoisie appeared in a few countries. To most Latin American elites the hopes of those who had urged such a pattern of development in the middle decades of the nineteenth century seemed in process of realization. They accepted evolutionary change which avoided both the perils of socialism and the colonial tradition of inefficient, privilege-granting government intervention and promised development with market forces as the main determinant of economic change and the role of government held to a minimum. A few Latin American analysts and the experience of the Mexican Revolution suggested that uncritical faith in such a developmental pattern was perhaps misplaced, that Latin America's future would not be a unilineal reproduction of what had occurred in parts of western Europe and in the United States which had evolved from earlier stages of raw material and foodstuff exports to industrial development. But the appearance in Mexico, Brazil, Colombia, Argentina, and Chile of industrial plants belied these doubts. Few took cognizance of the fact that European consumption of Latin American foodstuffs and some raw materials declined in the 1920's over prewar levels as European food production was stimulated to reduce imports.

The Great Depression and the Second World War forced Latin America to review not only its role as a peripheral economy to that of the industrial nations of the North Atlantic basin but also its faith in patterns of economic change without recourse to the revolutionary procedures undertaken in the Soviet Union, a backward area once considered—like Latin America—peripheral to the west European core economy. The magnitude of the depression which collapsed the international price level of Latin American exports and consequently posed a threat to national income and employment levels forced a reluctant review of the role of government in national economies. Government agencies intervened in the market to purchase agricultural, ranching, and mining output, to regulate exports or dispose of surplus, to supervise the volume and composition of imports, and to control the level and rates of exchange. To facilitate the supply of consumer goods which could no longer be obtained from foreign producers because of exchange shortages, governments assisted directly and indirectly the maintenance and expansion of established industrial units, financed the creation of new ones, and provided all the solicited levels of protection in the form of tariffs and exchange and import controls. These emergency measures, continued through the war years and afterward, were presumed part of the process of import-substitution, hopefully an acceleration of Latin America's unilineal evolution toward full industrialization, economic independence, and social change. In fact, the measures were *ad hoc* responses to uncoordinated pressures some from the traditional and others from the new sectors of the economy.

A number of factors underlay the new optimism at the end of the Second World War. From 1930 to 1945 temporary reduction in the capacity to import consumer finished goods provided a domestic market for national manufactures; added factors were tariff protection and population growth. Europe's post-war reconstruction and the demands of the Korean war fostered the belief that it was tenable to expect that the gains from international trade would provide exchange to finance long-delayed projects of industrial development and by mechanization to raise productivity in agriculture. The recession of British economic influence after 1945 led some to conclude that the long struggle against the "imperialism of free trade" for economic sovereignty would shortly be achieved. How else to interpret the results of

Péronist economic nationalism or Mexico's appropriation of foreign-owned oil companies? In sum, during the immediate post-war years changing international and national conditions indicated that Latin America would in the foreseeable future attain an appreciable degree of economic autonomy, by creating on a national scale a capital goods industry, developing and processing local sources of fuels, reducing foreign investment and raising local savings and investment rates, stimulating productivity not only in traditional export sectors but also in production of foodstuffs for internal consumption. Taken as a bloc these developments augured the achievement of economic autonomy, the end of economic dependence of the periphery upon the industrial core.

Since about 1955 developments, however, in Latin American society and economy have eroded the position of those who put their faith in change by evolution and have strengthened that of the structuralists—those believing that progress in Latin America requires radical change in economic policy, in the allocation and use of resources, in the distribution of income, in social policy, and in the nature and functioning of the political system. There is no doubt that the Cuban revolution in a country long considered an archetype of dependent economy and the resort there to socialism as the ideological basis for the achievement of political and economic autonomy produced ripples of self-examination throughout Latin America. It is equally undeniable that Cuban socialism induced the formulation of a neo-capitalistic alternative to socialism as an exit from Latin America's labyrinth of slow development—the Alliance for Progress. But the Cuban revolution and the minimal impact of the Alliance for Progress, while they created a wave of profound pessimism about the area's immediate future, only reinforced misgivings evident by the close of the Korean war and evolving independently of the Cuban phenomenon.

In the first place, the ability of Latin America's export-oriented economies to supply sustained dynamism to national development has been seriously weakened. For a variety of reasons the terms of trade or what Latin America's exports will purchase abroad have been unfavorable since about 1955 and some economists assert that such has been the long-term tendency of the area's exports. European purchasers of Latin America's exports have turned to their own ex-colonial or neo-colonial areas for the same products; or they have provided incentives to national production of once-imported foodstuffs, continuing a policy inaugurated in the 1920's; or their technology has reduced inputs of imported raw materials to maintain or increase output. In some exports, raw cotton, for example, Latin American exporters have had to compete with those of the United States in the world market. It should also be noted that the slow rate of population growth in the industrial areas of the North Atlantic basin and the operation of Engel's Law, or the low income elasticity of demand for food, according to which relative expenditure on food as a proportion of total income declines as per capita income grows, have also impeded the expansion of Latin America's primary product exports. Producers and shippers of traditional exports have had the wry satisfaction of heeding the advice of economists to maximize their comparative advantage in producing primary products and foodstuffs only to find the added volume is not compensated by comparable income increase and that the prospect for growth in demand for primary agricultural products is bleak.

Disappointing as has been the performance of the traditional export sector of the Latin American economy, its impact has been perhaps less than that of the present impasse of industrialization in most of the area, a condition which some observers have described as "the end of industrialization via import-substitution." Industrialization, many had long held, would have multiple effects: reduction of pressure on the balance of payments via domestic production of once imported finished goods; production of goods at prices lower than those of foreign manufactures thereby supplying a vast local market of the underprivileged; creation of an ever-growing demand for industrial labor and thus absorbing in gainful employment the pressures of rapid population growth; and ultimately by a process of industrial evolution leading to widespread industrial diversification, the establishment of a capital goods and intermediate goods industrial plant reducing dependence upon the core industrial area. Instead, by the 1960's, Latin American nations with the possible exception of Mexico (which once had *its* revolution) discovered that industrial production rose faster than industrial employment, that the demographic explosion could not be absorbed either by the agricultural, service, or industrial sectors. Moreover, a highly protected industry had fostered oligopoly and monopoly and a price structure for industrial goods whose supply was soon more than the domestic market could absorb. Most disturbing of all, the establishment of an efficient and viable basic industry required capital resources beyond public and private capabilities and a market greater than domestic consumers could provide. For this impasse of productive capacity greater than market size some economists urged regional trade integration, hitherto unsuccessful because opposed by national interests. Others viewed it as the seamless web of underdevelopment.

Poor performance in both agricultural and industrial sectors alone might be tolerated on the grounds that the present economic conjuncture, national and international, would improve in the long run. Complicating the situation and indeed creating an abiding sense of urgency, however, is the inescapable fact of an extraordinary rate of population growth which in the decade of the 1950's reached 2.7 per cent per year. The demands of a rapidly increasing population of low income and mounting expectations cannot long be neglected particularly when both urban and rural masses are becoming politicized. Even a rural labor force of extremely low per capita income can no longer be sustained under backward conditions of agricultural technology; in consequence domestic food supply lags behind potential demand, while rural migrants pour into cities whose services are inadequate. Efforts to absorb rural population in agricultural production have been hampered by failure to carry out much discussed plans of agrarian reform which, if passed by parliamentary bodies over the determined opposition of estate-owners, are seriously cut back in scope and hardly implemented. Vested interests in the traditional export sectors, moreover, are unwilling to have their economic power diminished.

Believers in the possibility that industrialization would emerge as a truly national enterprise financed and managed by national capital and a national bourgeoisie have seen their hopes dampened. A regressive tax system and the saving and consumption patterns of a tiny elite of high income have failed to provide investment commensurate with the requirements of modern industry. Under such circumstances foreign capital once largely confined to politically sensitive public services and the traditional export sectors has shifted into industrial enterprise. Further, the importation of industrial technology developed in the major industrial nations must be remunerated in the form of payments on patents and technical assistance furnished by the supranational corporations also located in the world's industrial core. In turn, the requirements of investment and technology beyond local possibilities have opened the way to the entry of foreign corporations, largely North American, into the domain of national industry, displacing the national bourgeoisie and leading to foreign control over domestic industrial enterprise. Faced by the pressure of the supranational corporations' resources in capital, technology, and entrepreneurial skills, the carefully nurtured nucleus of national industrial and financial bourgeoisie has sold them controlling interest in their enterprises, augmenting fears of "Americanization."

Ultimately socio-economic pressures must be resolved at the national level by representative bodies or by a dictatorial elite. In Latin America political systems have long been designed and maintained to limit popular demands. In many nations, high levels of illiteracy (between 40 and 50 per cent), weak peasant and industrial labor organizations, well-organized and highly influential landowning and business associations, the widespread use of political funds to influence voting, and finally the recourse to military force to destroy the results of elections—all have concentrated political control over national decision-making in the hands of a self-perpetuating elite or oligarchy whose decisions are governed by narrowly defined class interests rather than national considerations. In Latin America national governments are so only in name; in fact, they reflect the most powerful economic groups.

This highly summarized overview of main currents in

twentieth-century Latin America leads to the conclusion that the area as a bloc does not constitute a structure of society, economy, and politics perceptibly transformed beyond what was present at the end of the nineteenth century. Rather, it may be described with some accuracy as passing through a phase of mature neo-colonialism. So the structuralists argue that the presumed pattern of inevitable gradual evolution from a subsistence or closed economy through the stage of raw materials exports to full-scale industrial or open economy along the lines of England, Germany, the United States, and Japan is an illusion. These industrially dominant powers all passed through phases of imperialism and the mobilization of national resources human and natural for war whether one terms such preparations defensive or aggressive, phases still unknown in Latin America. For the structuralists of the peripheral economies of Latin America the evolutionary formula is based upon a general theory of economic development which embodies false concepts of universality. No underdeveloped economy and society, they insist, can be expected to become fully independent and autonomous in its decisions on vital areas of domestic policy because enduring neo-colonial structures since independence a century and a half ago have profoundly permeated the process of change and impede full-scale breakthrough to modernization. So they conclude that Latin America has not escaped its heritage of colonialism and neo-colonialism, that they are still prisoners rather than beneficiaries of the legacies of the past, that the terms "traditional," "colonial," "neo-colonial," or "developing" are in fact the same and that—as Hans Singer put it in 1951—"An underdeveloped country is like a giraffe—difficult to describe but you know one when you see one."

On Sources and Bibliography

A word about the origins of the major concepts advanced in preceding pages is in order before indicating some of the sources which the general reader may consult.

This synthesis is the outgrowth of two phases of research and teaching, the first devoted to the economic and social history of nineteenth-century Brazil, the second to research on the broader problem of Spain's trade with her American colonies. In the study of Brazil it was clear that plantation and slavery were the outgrowth of the colonial export economy and society and that twentieth-century Brazil did not escape that heritage. More important in clarifying the causes and development of dependence has been research in Mexican, Spanish, French, and British archives on Spain's colonial problem in America in the eighteenth and early nineteenth centuries. The concepts of dependence sketched out in this synthesis are derived largely from archival material, for it is in the manuscripts of governmental reports concerning metropolis and colonies that are found frank discussions of Spain's backwardness and underdevelopment vis-à-vis Europe's leading economic powers of the time, England and France, and of the role of the American colonies in the metropolitan economy. The printed sources—even the works of the so-called *proyectistas* or economic analysts of eighteenth-century Spain—tend to speak of dependence in far more guarded form. Dependence, however, is highlighted when insights derived from manuscript materials are applied to the published works.

In the same light the seventeenth-century analysts or *arbitristas* such as Sancho de Moncada and Manuel Lyra may be interpreted as discoursing on dependence, stagnation, backwardness. It should be emphasized that the economically advanced nations such as England and France did not publicize their dominant role in the Iberian nations, nor did the Iberians wish to publicize their inferiority. So there was preserved a community of silence on the structures of dependence tying colonies to Iberian metropolises to England and France, maintained for mutual benefit and different reasons.

Just as one is led backward in time in search of the origins of Iberian and Ibero-American structures of dependence, so one may follow their subsequent projection. Neo-colonial optimism tended to obscure the reality of dependence. In the twentieth century, some analysts have resumed the search for the causes of Latin America's backwardness and they tend to focus upon the persistence of the structures of dependence. In this fashion it has been possible to construct a framework of analysis for the broad trends of Latin American history from 1500 to 1900 and even beyond.

The titles that follow have been selected from the huge bibliography of French, English, Spanish, Portuguese, and German materials to suggest the basis of the interpretation of the development of Latin America's dependence. The bibliography is selective and suggestive. Preference has been given to works in English, and to recent syntheses. If these criteria are not met, works in other languages are cited. In view of the large and rapidly expanding bibliography on the social and economic history of Iberia and Ibero-American, sooner or later the interested reader must turn to the comprehensive bibliographical tools for generalist and specialist, the *Handbook of Latin American Studies* (1936–   ), the forthcoming Charles C. Griffin, ed., *Latin America. A Guide to Historical Literature,* and Benito Sánchez Alonso, *Fuentes de la historia de España e Hispano-América* (1952).

The Iberian Peninsula, 1500–1800

In recent years there have appeared comprehensive works dealing with the peninsular nations in the colonial period. They constitute more than "background" reading. First, however, should be mentioned the short and highly suggestive work by José Larraz López, *La época del mercantilismo en Castilla, 1500–1700* (2d. ed., 1943) which stresses Spain's inability to benefit by colonial expansion between 1500 and 1700. This theme is developed in detail for Portugal in Frédéric Mauro, *Le Portugal et l'Atlantique au XVIIe siècle, 1570–1670* (1960). Both should be read against the canvas of Jaime Vicens Vives, *An Economic History of Spain* (1969) which skillfully utilizes and interprets the classic and pioneer studies of Clarence Haring, *Trade and Navigation between Spain and the Indies in the Time of the Hapsburgs* (1918) and Earl P. Hamilton, *American Treasure and the Price Revolution in Spain, 1501–1650* (1934). Pierre and Huguette Chaunu have completed the most comprehensive study of one era of colonial trade, *Séville et l'Atlantique, 1504–1650* (1955–59). On foreign domination of the Spanish colonial system in its earliest phase see Ruth Pike, *Enterprise and Adventure. The Genoese in Seville and the Opening of the New World* (1966), in the seventeenth century, Albert Girard, *Le commerce français à Séville et à Cadix au temps des Habsbourgs* (1932), and at the end of the seventeenth, Erik W. Dahlgren, *Les rela-*

*tions commerciales et maritimes entre la France et les côtes de
l'océan Pacifique* (1909). For Spain in the sixteenth and seventeenth centuries there are John H. Elliot, *Imperial Spain, 1469–
1716* (1963), John Lynch, *Spain under the Habsburgs* (1964) and
volumes II and III of Jaime Vicens Vives, ed., *Historia económica y social de España y América* (1957–59). One must savor
the classic description of an underdeveloped economy and society
in the grip of inflation in Pierre Vilar, "Le temps de Quichotte,"
Europe (1956) and reprinted in his *Crecimiento y desarrollo*
(1964). Indispensable for comparative economic and social development in C. Hill's volume on England, *The Century of
Revolution, 1603–1714* (1961).

Basic for an understanding of the economic, social, and intellectual currents of the eighteenth century are volume IV of
Vicens Vives, ed., *Historia económica,* Richard Herr, *The
Eighteenth Century Revolution in Spain* (1958), Jean Sarrailh,
L'Espagne éclairée de la seconde moitié du XVIIIe siècle (1954)
and Robert J. Shafer, *The Economic Societies in the Spanish
World, 1763–1821* (1958). A series of articles by J. Muñoz Pérez
on Spanish economic thought of the seventeenth and eighteenth
centuries, based upon intensive archival research and indicating
the importance of the American colonies to Spanish renovation
in the eighteenth century are indispensable: "La publicación del
reglamento de comercio libre de Indias de 1778," *Anuario de
estudios americanos,* IV (1947), 615-64; "Los proyectos sobre
España e Indias en el siglo XVIII: el proyectismo como género,"
Revista de estudios políticos, no. 81 (1955), 169-85; "El comercio
de Indias bajo los Austrias y la crítica del proyectismo del
XVIII," *Anuario de estudios americanos,* XIII (1956), 1–83; "El
comercio de Indias bajo los Austrias y los tratadistas españoles
del siglo XVII, *"Revista de Indias,* XVII (1957), 209-21.

On the wider importance of the Iberian colonies in America to
European trade, a much underemphasized factor in eighteenth-
century economic development, there are D. A. Fairnie, "Commercial Empire of the Atlantic, 1607-1783," *Economic History*

Review, XV (1962), 205-18, H. E. S. Fisher, "Anglo-Portuguese Trade, 1700–1750," *Economic History Review,* XVI (1963), 219-33, Allan Christelow, "Great Britain and the Trades from Cadiz and Lisbon to Spanish America and Brazil, 1759–1783," *Hispanic American Historical Review,* XXVII (1947), 2-29, Gaston Rambert, "La France et la politique commerciale de l'Espagne au XVIIIe siècle," *Revue d'histoire moderne et contemporaine,* VI (1959), 269–88, and Kenneth Maxwell, "Pombal and the Nationalization of the Luso-Brazilian Economy," *Hispanic American Historical Review* XLVIII (1968), 608-31.

The Ibero-American Colonies, 1500–1800

Sweeping through both colonial and modern times is the classic article by Sanford Mosk, "Latin America versus the United States," reprinted in Lewis Hanke, ed., *Do the Americas have a Common History?* (1964), 165-87. For materials on Amerindian culture there are (Mesoamerica) Eric Wolf, *Sons of the Shaking Earth* (1959), (Mexico) Charles Gibson, *The Aztecs under Spanish Rule* (1964), (Peru) John Rowe, "Inca Culture at the Time of the Spanish Conquest," and George Kubler, "The Quechua in the Colonial World," in volume II of the *Handbook of South American Indians,* edited by Julian H. Steward (1946). A good overview is also in Julian H. Steward and Louis C. Faron, *Native Peoples of South America* (1959). A critical review of Spanish Indian policy is in John Rowe, "The Incas under Spanish Colonial Institutions," *Hispanic American Historical Review,* XXXII (1957), 155-99.

The work of Sherburne Cook and Woodrow Borah on the demography of Central Mexico until about 1650 is a major contribution to the social history of the colonial period. Their findings are in University of California, Berkeley, *Iberoamericana,* nos. 31, 35, 43, 44, 45, 50. Their results should be compared with Angel Rosenblat, *La población indígena y el mestizaje en América* (1954) and the same author's *La población de América en*

1492. Viejos y nuevos cálculos (1967). A recent review of population levels over time is H. F. Dobyns, "Estimating American Population," *Current Anthropology,* VII (1966), 395-460.

François Chevalier has interwoven settlement patterns, economic activity, and social structure in *Land and Society in Colonial Mexico. The Great Hacienda* (1963); of comparable perception is James Lockhart, *Spanish Peru, 1532-1560* (1968). For Brazil a publication of broader scope is Caio Prado, Jr., *The Colonial Background of Modern Brazil* (1967) which should be supplemented by C. R. Boxer, *The Dutch in Brazil* (1957) and Dauril Alden, *Royal Government in Colonial Brazil* (1968). As for race relations in Ibero-America, Magnus Mörner has surveyed and admirably synthesized the literature in *Race Mixture in the History of Latin America* (1967).

A wealth of basic detail, thoughtful synthesis and the results of the most recent scholarship are to be found in John H. Parry, *The Spanish Seaborne Empire* (1966), Charles Gibson, *Spain in America* (1966) and Silvio Zavala, *El mundo americano en la época colonial* (1968). Gibson's excellent bibliographical essay will direct those interested to bibliographical tools, source materials, and recent secondary publications on colonial society, economy, and political institutions.

Neo-colonial Latin America: The Nineteenth Century

A number of publications highlight socio-economic factors in the wars of independence. Illustrative of the polemical literature of the time of the wars are A. Flores Estrada, *Examen imparcial de las disensiones de la América con España* (1812) and William Walton, *An Exposé on the Dissensions of Spanish America* (1914). More recently, there have appeared stimulating treatments of these factors in Charles C. Griffin, "Economic and Social Aspects of the Era of Spanish-American Independence," *Hispanic American Historical Review,* XXIX (1949), 170-87 and in the materials selected and introduced by Robin A. Humphreys and John Lynch, *The Origins of the Latin American Revolutions, 1808–1826* (1965). The continuity of colonial institutions in post-colonial Latin America is sketched out suggestively in a symposium, Woodrow Borah, Charles Gibson, and Robert Potash, "Colonial Institutions and Contemporary Latin America," *Hispanic American Historical Review*, XLIII (1963), 371-94.

Before examining the national literature on nineteenth-century developments, the reader is advised to dip into recently published materials oriented toward contemporary Latin America which emphasize the continuity of the structures of dependence. Those emphasizing economic factors include Sanford Mosk, "Latin American and the World Economy, 1850–1914," *Inter-American Economic Affairs*, II (1948), 53-82, and two contributions by Raúl Prebisch, *The Economic Development of Latin America and its Principal Problems* (1950) and *Towards a Dynamic Development Policy for Latin America* (1964). To these must be added Alberto Baltra Cortés, *Crecimiento económico de América Latina: problemas fundamentales* (3d ed., 1961) Gustavo Beyhaut, *Raíces contemporáneas de América Latina* (1964) and Celso Furtado, *Subdesarrollo y estancamiento en América Latina* (1966). Further, a number of interdisciplinary collaborative volumes have pinpointed the shortcomings of contemporary Latin America and in the process they suggest their historical roots. Among many are two volumes edited by Claudio Veliz, *Obstacles to Change in Latin America* (1965) and *The Politics of Conformity in Latin America* (1967), James Petras and Maurice Zeitlin, eds., *Latin America. Reform or Revolution?* (1968), Albert Hirschman, ed., *Latin American Issues: Essays and Comments* (1961), Charles Wagley, ed., *Social Science Research on Latin America* (1964) and its companion piece, Manuel Diegues, Jr., and Bryce Wood, eds., *Social Science in Latin America* (1967). Finally, there is Charles Griffin's compact survey of Latin America at the end of the century in *The New Cambridge Modern History*, XI (1962), Chapter XIX, while the political and intellectual dimensions of post-colonial developments are covered by the participants in W. W. Pierson, ed., "The Pathology of Democracy in Latin America," *American Political Science Review,* XLIV (1950), 100-49, and by Leopoldo Zea, *The Latin American Mind* (1963); exceptionally rich in insight is Jacques Lambert, *Latin America: Social Structure and Political Institutions* (1967).

Argentina

Useful introductions to the social and economic history of Argentina in the nineteenth century are Ysabel F. Rennie, *The Argentina Republic* (1945) and the appropriate chapter in Harry Bernstein, *Modern and Contemporary Latin America* (1952). Groups and factors in regional conflict or what is called today internal war are discussed in Juan Álvarez, *Estudio sobre las guerras civiles argentinas y el problema de Buenos Aires en la república* (3d ed., 1936), Jacinto Oddone, *El factor económico en nuestras luchas civiles* (1937) and the classic analysis of Miron Burgin, *Economic Aspects of Argentine Federalism, 1820–1852* (1946). Sectoral analyses are found in James Scobie, *Revolution on the Pampas: a Social History of Argentine Wheat, 1860–1910* (1964), and Horacio Giberti, *Historia económica de la ganadería argentina* (1954). A broader canvas of economic change appears in Roberto Cortés Conde and Ezequiel Gallo, *La formación de la Argentina moderna* (1967), H. S. Ferns, *Britain and Argentina in the Nineteenth Century* (1960) and Raúl Scalabrini Ortiz, *Política británica en el Río de la Plata* (1940). Jorge M. Mayer's *Alberdi y su tiempo* (1963) examines comprehensively the life and time of a man who recognized the interrelationship of policy and economic development while José L. Romero's *A History of Argentine Political Thought* (1963) relates social change to political ideology.

Brazil

Two volumes furnish an introduction to economic change in
nineteenth-century Brazil: Caio Prado, Jr., *Historia económica
do Brasil* (8th ed., 1963) and the more theoretically oriented,
Celso Furtado, *The Economic Growth of Brazil* (1963). Imperialist pressure and the influence of a modern upon a backward culture are examined in A. K. Manchester, *British pre-
eminence in Brazil: Its Rise and Decline. A Study in European
Expansion* (1933), Richard Graham, *Britain and the Onset of
Modernisation in Brazil, 1850–1914* (1968) and Gilberto Freyre,
*Os ingleses no Brasil. Aspectos da influencia británica sobre a
vida, a paisagem e a cultura do Brasil* (1948).

Social as well as socio-economic analyses are especially prominent in Brazilian studies and have provided no little insight
into the process whereby neo-colonialism has endured. After the
general studies of Charles Wagley, *An Introduction to Brazil*
(1963) and Gilberto Freyre, *The Mansions and the Shanties.
The Making of Modern Brazil* (1963), the reader may proceed
to the narrower studies of the structures of slavery and their
legacy in Stanley J. Stein, *Vassouras, a Brazilian Coffee County,
1850–1900* (1957), Fernando Henrique Cardoso, *Capitalismo e
escravidão no Brasil meridional: o negro na sociedade escravo-
crata do Rio Grande do Sul* (1962), Octavio Ianni, *As meta-
morfoses do escravo: apogeu e crise da escravidão no Brasil
meridional* (1962) and Emilia Viotti da Costa, *Da senzala à
colônia* (1966). Marvin Harris, *Patterns of Race in the Americas*
(1964) takes issue with the "humanitarian" thesis of Latin American slavery and offers an explanation for the absorption of
Negro freedmen. The absorption and the adaptation of European
ideological currents are traced in João Cruz Costa, *A History
of Ideas in Brazil* (1964).

Economic and social factors of backwardness are reviewed in

their political context in the volumes on the nineteenth century of Sergio Buarque de Holanda, ed., *Historia geral da civilização brasileira* (1960–   ) and José Maria Bello, *A History of Modern Brazil, 1889-1964* (1966), which contains more on the nineteenth century than the title indicates. The political processes of neo-colonialism are described in Victor Nunes Leal, *Coronelismo, enxada e voto. O municipio e o regime representativo no Brasil* (1945), José Honorio Rodriguez, *Conciliação e reforma no Brasil: um desafio historico-cultural* (1965) and Paula Beiguelman, *Formação politica do Brasil* (1967).

Mexico

By comparison with most countries of Latin America, social and economic history of the nineteenth century has attracted considerable attention in Mexico. Luis Villoro, *La revolución de independencia. Ensayo de interpretación historica* (1953) seeks to relate interest groups and political factions during the revolution, as does Luis Chávez Orozco, *Historia económica y social de Mexico. Ensayo de interpretación* (1938) for the period 1820–1840. The attempt to create a textile industry and its limited success is explored by Robert Potash, *El banco de avio de Mexico. El fomento industrial, 1821-1841* (1959) and Jan Bazant's contribution in *La industria nacional y el comercio exterior, 1842-1851* (1862) published by the Banco Nacional de Comercio Exterior. Jan Bazant, "La desamortisación de los bienes corporativos de 1856," *Historia mexicana*, XVI, 193-212 is a major contribution to the study of the sale and distribution of church holdings. The intellectual and political manifestations of the heritage of colonialism is examined in the three volumes of Jesús Reyes Heroles, *El liberalismo mexicano* (1957-61) and in a more critical vein in Charles A. Hale, *Mexican Liberalism in the Age of Mora, 1821-1853* (1968). The extent to which factionalism had shattered neo-colonial Mexico and opened the way to U.S. imperialism is Mariano Otero's, *Consideraciones sobre la situación política y social de la república mexicana en el año de 1847* (1848).

The Indian and the mestizo in neo-colonial Mexico is the subject of Moisés Gonzalez Navarro, "Instituciones indígenas en Mexico independiente," in Instituto Indigenista Nacional, *Métodos y resultados de la política indigenista en Mexico* (1954); an earlier treatment of the same theme of social and political change but on a wider scope is Andrés Molina Enriquez, *Los grandes problemas nacionales* (1909).

Outstanding studies of Mexico's social and economic history of the latter part of the nineteenth century and, in particular, of the expansion of the hacienda and its effects upon the rural population are found in volumes II-IV and VII of Daniel Cosío Villegas, ed., *Historia moderna de Mexico* (1955–   ). In addition the reader will wish to review the opening sections of Frank Tannenbaum, *The Mexican Agrarian Revolution* (1929) and Raymond Vernon, *The Dilemma of Mexico's Development. The Roles of the Public and Private Sectors* (1963). Finally, the intellectual counterpart of laisser faire development in neo-colonial Mexico is treated extensively in Leopoldo Zea, *Apogeo y decadencia del positivismo en Mexico* (1944), a shorter form of which appeared in F. S. C. Northrop, *Ideological Differences and World Order. Studies in the Philosophy and Science of the World's cultures* (1949).

Index

Abolition: in Brazil, 149-50; in
Venezuela, 163
Absolutism, rejected as model after
independence, 168
Agriculture: in England, 5; in
Spain, 16; in Spanish colonies
(1500-1700), 28, 30, 31-39; in
Portuguese colonies, 22-24,
39-43; pre-Columbian, 32-35;
export, in colonial Latin
America, 39-44; food output of,
in 20th century, 196. *See also*
Coffee; Estancia; Export
economy; Fazenda; Planta-
tion; Land tenure; Sugar.
Amerinds: labor of, 23, 29, 32,
41-42, 49, 78-80, 127-28, 174,
177-78; pre-Conquest agriculture of, 32-35; demography
of, 32, 33-34, 37-38, 65, 165,
178; pre-Conquest societies of,
in Mesoamerica and Central
Andes, 34-36; tribute of, 35, 36;
communities of, 38, 39, 62,
139, 162, 177; maligned by
Consulado of Mexico, 56-57; in
colonial society, 57-59; and
Spanish trade, 78; 19th century policy toward, 161-62,
177-79. *See also* Caciques; Indigenismo; Race; Racism; Rebellions.
Argentina: regionalism in, 133;
estancias of, 136, 145-46; constitution of 1853, 145. *See also*
Rio de la Plata.

16; in Spanish colonial economy (1700), 28-29; in Spanish economy and society, 44-45; loss of, to Spain by contraband and privateering, 45; and price-fixing in colonial trade of Spain, 48; and Banco de San Carlos, 100; England seeks Mexican, 108. *See also* Mining.

Slave trade: English in, 8; Portuguese in, 23; United States in Brazilian, 149-50; Brazil ends, 149, 163; to Cuba, 163; as factor in independence, 163

Slavery: of Africans in Brazilian agriculture, 23, 39, 42; of Amerinds in Brazil, 23, 41-42; and plantation agriculture in America, 40; and society of castes, 59; in Brazil, compared with condition of labor in Europe, 79; and Roman Catholic Church, 116-17; and status of labor in colonial heritage, 117-18; rationalization of, 118-19, 129; attacked in Brazil in 1820's, 148; factors of decline and abolition of, in Brazil, 149-50; in prolongation of Cuban status as colony and of Brazilian monarchy, 164; and republican institutions, 168, 172

Social change, controlled by elites in 19th century, 160-66

Social Darwinism, and racism, 184

Social mobility: of Spaniards in Reconquest and Conquest, 20, 30, 58, 71; "passing," integration and co-optation in, 117-18; controlled by elites in 19th century, 160-66; of bourgeois and middle class, 168-69; of educated European immigrants, 175; barriers to, 177-79; of Brazilian mulattoes, 180-82; of mestizos in 19th century, 182

Social stratification, mechanisms of, 174-77

Society: Spanish (1500-1700), 17-20; pre-Columbian, in Central America and Central Andes 34-36; colonial, 37-39, 57-64, 114, 115; Spanish, webbed by colonial interests, 45-46, 71-72; 19th century Latin American, 174-85. *See also* Family; Population; Race; Social mobility.

Spain: as economic dependency of Europe, 4, 15, 16, 17; dependence of, on colonies, 12, 30-31, 44-45; economic growth and contraction of (1500-1700), 12-20, 28; as patrimonial state, 13-15, 69-70; under Bourbons, 89-99, 101, 103-4; alliance of, with France, 11, 102, 104; and French Revolution, 104; alliance of, with England (1793-95), 104, 108; Bourbons of, abdicate (1808), 105; political crisis in, and colonial problem (1807-10), 106-13. *See also*